PHONEMIC AWARENESS

Playing with Sounds to Strengthen Beginning Reading Skills

Written by

Jo Fitzpatrick

Contributing Writers:

Karen Bauer
Carol Dietzschold
Rosa Drew
Marcia Fries
Terry Petersen

Illustrator:

Catherine Yuh

Editor:

Karen P. Hall

Project Director:

Carolea Williams

CTP ©1997 Creative Teaching Press, inc., Cypress, CA 90630

Table of Contents

Letter from the Author 4

Phonemic-Awareness Overview 5

   What Is Phonemic Awareness?
   Phonemic Awareness and Phonics
   Why Teach Phonemic Awareness?
   How Is Phonemic Awareness Taught?

Levels of Phonemic Awareness 8

Extending Phonemic Awareness into Written Language 13

Parent Letters 15

**Phonemic-Awareness Activities
Practice Before Print**

1 Level 1

   Seeing Sounds 19
   Nursery-Rhyme Rattle 19
   Getting to Know You 20
   "Buggie" Boxes 20
   Rhyme Time 21
   What's My Sound? 21
   Rhyme Away 22
   Draw a Rhyme 22
   No Zoo for You! 23
   Silly Willy Song 23
   Did You Ever? 24
   Oddball Out 24
   Clap, Snap, or Tap? 25
   Rhythm Time March 25
   Rhyming Picture Sort 26
   Sing a Song of Sounds 26
   Silly Greetings 27
   Hink Pink 27

2 Level 2

   Who Did You Catch? 28
   Start and Stop 28
   Punch It Out 29
   Break It in Half 29
   Turtle Talk 30
   Key to the Code 30
   Bubble-Gum Words 31
   Name Chant 31
   The Sounds in the Word 32
   Patty-Cake Sounds 32
   Talking Ghost 33
   Mystery Box 33
   Pop-Up People 34

3 Level 3

   Sound Bingo 34
   Web of Sounds 35
   Mystery Trip 35
   Sound Train 36
   Sound Dominos 36
   What Big Ears You Have! 37
   Puppet Pop-Ups 37
   Where's That Sound? 38
   What Do You Hear? 38
   What Is It? 39
   Thumbs Up! 39
   Give It the Test 40
   Three in a Row 40
   Bag of Sounds 41
   Scavenger Hunt 41
   Grab Bag .42
   Catch the Sound 42
   Listen Up! 43
   Picture Spelling 43
   Color-Coded Sounds 44
   Penny Push 44

4 Level 4

I Spy 45
Tap and Sweep 45
Count the Sounds 46
Classifying Objects 46
Sound Baseball 47
Jump to the Sounds 47
Tap to the Sounds 48
Eat Your Words 48
Put It Together, Take It Apart 49
Froggy Hop 49
Echoes 50
Begin with Green 50
Head, Waist, Toes 51
Word-Family Trees 51
All Aboard the Sound Train 52

5 Level 5

Zippity-Bippity 52
Animal Fun 53
Circle Around the Sound 53
Change Your Partner 54
Drop Off, Add On 54

Moving into Print

1 Level 1

Simon Says Sounds 55
We Are Family 55
Letter Hunt 56

2 Level 2

Letter Patterns 56
Monster Puppets 57
Walkie-Talkie Friends 57
Slip and Slide 58
Choo-Choo Charlie 58
Picture Puzzles 59
Be the Sound 59
Word Line .60

3 Level 3

Sort by Sound 60
Color-Coded Reading 61
Photo Line 61
Sound Relay 62
Word Chain 62

4 5 Levels 4 and 5

Friendship Directory 63
Word Detectives 63
Change That Vowel! 64
Sound Switch 64
Rhyming Zig-Zag 65
Word-Family Race 65
Alphabet House 66
Build a Word 66

Reproducibles and Resources 67

Recommended Books 126

Letter from the Author

Dear Readers,

Because I have been "retained" in first grade for well over 20 years, I've learned first-hand the importance of phonemic awareness. This aptitude either "opens the door" and welcomes children to a new world of reading, or it slams that door shut, leaving them "outside" and unable to function in their reading environment. Many times, beginning readers struggle because they lack the thousands of hours of "prereading prerequisites" many of their peers have experienced. Phonemic awareness is the key that allows these children to understand how the reading world works—to reach out, open the door, and confidently walk into the world of reading.

This book has been designed to help students develop a working knowledge as well as a conscious understanding of how language works. The activities and games have been implemented in prereading and emergent classes with astonishing success. They are presented developmentally, based on the five levels of phonemic awareness. Many activities are oral in nature, but can be readily adapted to written language. *Do not expect mastery*—phonemic awareness is an ability that takes time and practice to develop. Individual progress will vary, and students will be helped more by a variety of experiences than by repeated drills. Frequent but intermittent repetition is much more beneficial.

Finally, keep in mind that the following phonemic-awareness activities are "generic" in nature, and any list of appropriate words can be used. Ideally, words taken from current classroom literature (e.g., read-aloud or shared reading books) are best—they allow students to focus on the auditory, visual, and/or structural aspects of key words before beginning guided reading. As a result, phonemic awareness will be effortlessly, but effectively, integrated into the core reading program.

I sincerely hope this resource on phonemic awareness serves as a springboard for learning, and that many more excellent literacy-promoting ideas and experiences evolve.

Jo Fitzpatrick

Jo Fitzpatrick

Phonemic-Awareness Overview

What Is Phonemic Awareness?

Students need to have a strong understanding of spoken language before they can understand written language. This knowledge of how language works is called *phonemic awareness.* Phonemic awareness is not a skill. It is the ability

- to examine language independent of meaning (hear the sounds that make up the words).

- to attend to sounds in the context of a word (see relationships between sounds).

- to manipulate component sounds (alter and rearrange sounds to create new words).

The significance of phonemic awareness lies not in the ability to recognize differences in sounds (phonemes), but in knowing these sounds are manipulative elements of our language. Children need to be able to hear sounds, know their positions, and understand the role they play within a word. For example, say, /s/ (the sound of the letter, not the name). Now slowly say, *see* and *so,* paying close attention to the formation of your mouth when you say the words. Even though both words begin with the same letter, the /s/ sound is slightly different. As /s/ is pronounced, it is done in anticipation of the vowel that follows, changing the oral sound of the phoneme.

The path to phonemic awareness is sequential, beginning with awareness of spoken words, then to syllables, followed by onsets and rimes*, and finally to individual sounds within a word. This awareness is not innate, it must be acquired. The key to developing strong phonological awareness lies in training and practice. As students progress through different phonemic-awareness levels, they become proficient at listening for and reproducing sounds they hear, or listening "inside" words. Phonemic-awareness instruction helps children understand, use, and apply oral language.

* An *onset* is all of the sounds in a word that come before the first vowel. A *rime* is the first vowel in a word and all the sounds that follow. (For example, in the word *splint,* the onset is *spl-* and the rime is *-int.*)

Phonemic Awareness and Phonics

Phonemic awareness and phonics are not the same but are mutually dependent. Phonemic awareness focuses on the sound units (phonemes) used to form spoken words; phonics instruction associates sounds to written symbols (i.e., the alphabet). Together, they help children develop word-recognition skills, namely the ability to "sound out" unknown words. Once beginning readers have mastered sound-symbol relationships and applied them to print, they can approximate the pronunciation of most printed words.

Before phonics can be taught, phonemic awareness is essential. Children must be able to hear and manipulate oral sound patterns before they can relate them to print. Phonics instruction builds on a child's ability to segment and blend together sounds he or she hears. Without this ability, children have difficulty with basic decoding skills—an integral component of any reading program.

Studies show that connections between oral language and print must be thoroughly developed to achieve reading success. Reading programs that include systematic instruction on letter-to-sound correspondence lead to higher achievement, both in word recognition and spelling. In other words, a prereader's knowledge of letters and their names is important, but not enough. Familiarity with letters, combined with a sensitivity to phonetic structure, is essential for early reading success.

Why Teach Phonemic Awareness?

Children in the early stages of language development have difficulty sequencing sounds. Many times a word is heard as just one big sound, as their understanding of the alphabetic principle is limited. It is essential, however, for the progression to phonics and reading, that children are able to hear sounds and the patterns used to make up words. Before children can identify a letter that stands for a sound, they must be able to hear that individual sound in a word. This is a difficult task, as sounds (phonemes) are abstract in nature.

For example, when we say the word *dog*, the three distinct sounds that form the word are not heard separately—the phonemes are not auditorally divisible. The only way the sounds /d/ /o/ /g/ are heard is by thinking of them separately, one at a time. This segmenting of sounds does not come easily. It takes training and modeling before students are capable of thinking of sounds separately within a word. Once students can identify individual sounds, they can break the word into separate phonemic elements and manipulate them within the context of the word.

Students need to know phonemic sounds, but it is vital to successful decoding (reading) and encoding (spelling) that they know how to apply their phonological skills. Studies show that an absence of phonemic awareness is characteristic of students who are failing, or have failed, to learn to read. The implication is clear—phonemic awareness can significantly bridge the critical gap between inadequate preparation for literacy and success in beginning reading.

How Is Phonemic Awareness Taught?

The goal of phonemic awareness is to help children develop an "ear" for language—to hear specific sounds, identify sound sequence, and understand the role phonemes play in word formation. Although it can have visual overtones, phonemic awareness is basically oral in nature and presents itself well in meaningful, interactive games and activities.

Phonemic awareness is multi-leveled and progresses through five sequential stages. (See *Levels of Phonemic Awareness*, pages 8–12, for a detailed explanation of each phonemic-awareness level.) Before starting instruction, it is important to assess students to determine their awareness level. This helps indicate where your instruction should begin and what areas need emphasis. The Phonemic-Awareness Inventory (pages 67–69) is a comprehensive tool that assesses students' phonological performance. This assessment should be given orally and individually to each child. (You may choose to use parent volunteers or instructional assistants to help administer assessments.)

After assessment, use the activities and reproducibles to help promote stronger phonemic knowledge. These activities are designed to help students develop a working knowledge as well as a conscious understanding of how language works. They are grouped in two categories—those that are oral or pictorial in nature (pages 19–54), and those involving letter recognition and sound/symbol relationships (pages 55–66). Within each category, activities are arranged according to level of difficulty. Photocopy, laminate, and cut activity pages into half-size sheets for easy use and storage.

As you teach phonemic awareness, keep in mind that it is not an isolated skill. For meaningful reading development, phonological training should be incorporated into current reading materials or programs. The goal is integrated practice, so when doing the activities, choose vocabulary related to a current story or theme.

Levels of Phonemic Awareness

The activities in this book are grouped according to the following levels of phonemic awareness. Review this information thoroughly before assessing students' abilities and incorporating phonemic-awareness activities into your reading program.

Level 1
Rhythm and Rhyme

At level one, children develop an "ear" for language. They hear, identify, and match similar word patterns (e.g., rhymes, alliterations). They also listen for, detect, and count syllables within words. The goal is to help children develop stronger auditory discrimination and awareness. Exposure and experience are the keys to mastering this level by comparing and contrasting the overall sounds in words.

TASKS

- **Hearing and identifying similar word patterns (sound matching)**

- **Listening for and detecting spoken syllables (syllable counting)**

Instruction Guidelines

Read many stories aloud, especially those containing rhyming words (e.g., *cat, bat*) and alliterations (e.g., *Peter Piper picked a peck of pickled peppers*). Use both auditory and visual learning devices (e.g., chants, songs, picture cards, puppets) to help students focus on and compare sound patterns. Have children listen for, tap out, and count syllables in spoken words. Syllables are acoustically and articulatorily distinct in the flow of oral language, making them easier to identify and distinguish than individual letter sounds (phonemes).

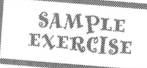

SAMPLE EXERCISE

Say words pairs (e.g., *fox, box; bear, chair; horse, house*), and ask children to identify those that rhyme. Have more advanced learners think of a rhyming word to match a given word.

LEVEL 2

Level 2
Parts of a Word

At level two, children listen for sounds within a word. They discover that speech can be broken down into smaller "sound units"—words to syllables, syllables to onsets and rimes, and onsets and rimes to phonemes. They experiment with oral synthesis, blending sounds together to form spoken words.

Oral synthesis is the backbone of decoding—it focuses on hearing sounds in sequence and blending them together to make a word. Oral synthesis contains all the challenges of phonetic decoding except letter recognition. This skill provides support for the least prepared children who have no concept of words or sounds—it also helps them understand the alphabetic principle.

Instruction Guidelines

Begin by having children blend together onsets and rimes—the "sound units" derived from splitting syllables. For example, say *sp–ill* to form the word *spill*. It is much easier for children to hear the distinction between onsets and rimes than to hear separate phonemic components. Once students have mastered identifying and blending onsets and rimes, proceed to phoneme blending—combining sounds that correspond to individual letters or graphemes (e.g., */s/–/p/–/i/–/l/* to form the word *spill*).

> ### SAMPLE EXERCISE
>
> **Segment sounds by saying them slowly, separating individual sounds. Use two-phoneme words first (e.g., */i/–/s/, /a/–/t/, /u/–/p/*), followed by three- and four-phoneme words divided into onsets and rimes (e.g., *m–an, c–at, sl–eep*). As student abilities improve, move to completely segmented words (e.g., */j/–/ee/–/p/, /b/–/ar/–/k/, /sh/–/i/–/p/*).**

> ### TASKS
>
> - **Identifying onsets and rimes (syllable splitting)**
> - **Blending individual sounds to form a word (phoneme blending)**

Focus on blending sounds rather than taking words apart—splitting words into phonemes requires more knowledge and insight (see Level 4) than simply combining "strange little sounds" together to form a word. Say words slowly, stretching out and enunciating each separate sound. Have children blend the sounds together to identify the word.

Level 3
Sequence of Sounds

Students in the early stages of phonemic development have difficulty sequencing sounds. Many times a word will sound like one big sound, especially when knowledge of the alphabet is limited. At level three, children direct their attention to specific positions of sounds within a word. This is early training for segmenting sounds independently. Once recognition of beginning, middle, and ending sounds is acquired, children are better able to isolate sounds and hear them separately.

TASKS

- **Identifying where a given sound is heard in a word (approximation)**

- **Identifying beginning, middle, and ending sounds in a word (phoneme isolation)**

Instruction Guidelines

Begin by identifying a target sound, then say words and have children identify whether the sound is heard at the beginning, middle, or end of the word. Children do not have to know the names of letters to master this level—the emphasis is on *listening*, not letter recognition. Have them repeat the sound heard, not the letter name, when identifying phonemes.

SAMPLE EXERCISE

Say the word *book* and ask children, *What sound did you hear first?* (/b/). After a correct response, continue with beginning and middle sounds. Repeat with other words, having children randomly identify the beginning, middle, and ending sounds. After further practice, change the format by giving the directive first, followed by the words (e.g., *Listen to these words and tell me what sound you hear at the end of the word*).

What is the last sound you hear in the word "mouse"?

LEVEL 4

Level 4
Separation of Sounds

By this level, children have acquired a good sense of phonemic awareness and are ready to acoustically divide words into separate sounds or phonemes. This skill is reverse of phoneme blending, where "sound units" are combined (see Level 2). While separation of sounds (phoneme segmentation) appears to be a simple feat, many children, even older ones, struggle with this skill. They may be able to identify isolated sounds (recognition), but cannot break a word into separate phonemic components.

TASKS

- **Counting the number of phonemes in a word (phoneme counting)**

- **Identifying individual sounds within a word (phoneme segmentation)**

Instruction Guidelines

Before attempting to split apart and identify individual phonemes, have children count the number of sounds in a word. Say each word slowly as children listen for, tap out, and count the number of phonemes they hear. After they master this skill, move on to the more difficult task of identifying individual phonemes. (Remember to have children repeat the individual sounds they hear, not letter names.)

SAMPLE EXERCISE

Say two- and three-phoneme words one at a time. Ask children to orally separate the sounds so that each phoneme is repeated. For example, *no /n/–/o/, up /u/–/p/, egg /e/–/g/, bit /b/–/i/–/t/.*

There are three sounds in the word "tree."

Level 5
Manipulation of Sounds

Level five is the highest level of phonemic awareness. Children manipulate sounds within words—adding, exchanging, deleting, or transposing phonemes to form new words. Students should have solid knowledge of how language works before attempting this level. They should be adept at mentally blending sounds, modifying words, and segmenting sounds in order to make the phonemic transference. The ability to manipulate phonemes strongly correlates with beginning reading acquisition.

TASKS

- Substituting beginning, middle, and ending sounds of a word (phoneme substitution)

- Omitting beginning, middle, and ending sounds of a word (phoneme deletion)

Instruction Guidelines

Begin by having children add, substitute, or delete beginning consonant sounds. Working with initial consonant sounds is an easier task to master than modifying ending sounds (i.e., it is easier for children to identify the /p/ in *pat* than the /p/ in *tap*). Once students have mastered manipulation of beginning consonant sounds, advance to ending sounds and then middle sounds.

SAMPLE EXERCISE

Give the oral directive, *Say* cat *without the /c/.* After a correct response, continue with other examples (e.g., pan *without /p/,* fit *without /f/*). After sufficient practice, increase the difficulty by giving children less specific directions (e.g., *Leave off the first sound in these words; Can you move the sounds around in the word* eat *to come up with a different word?*).

Extending Phonemic Awareness into Written Language

When learning to read, children associate sounds with printed words. When presented with a written word, children must readily see the word as a unit, with letters combining together to make one sound (e.g., the word *dog* is read as one blended "unit"). Having become accustomed to hearing letter sounds, moving into written letter combinations and sentence formation can be challenging for young learners. To ease this transition, students should be "overly exposed" to letters and their combination patterns.

Before children can understand the alphabetic principle (that letters have names and sounds, and sounds make up words), they need to understand that letters are more than just random symbols. When combined in specific ways, like pieces of a puzzle, letters are tools to communicate with others.

Using simple geometric shapes that demonstrate "parts making up the whole" can help children visualize this abstract concept. Draw pictures of common objects (e.g., circle, pencil, rainbow, kite), and cut them into pieces. Show children that as separate pieces, objects are difficult to identify—the "message" is unclear. But when pieces are put together in the right order, much like letters in words, the "picture" is clear—we understand the information being presented.

After children have manipulated geometric shapes and are comfortable with the notion of letters as "parts" that make up the whole (words), expand the concept into letter combinations. Allow children to freely explore and manipulate letters (e.g., plastic letters, sponge letters, alphabet puzzle pieces, alphabet cards), and discuss how some letter combinations form words that make sense, while others form "nonsense" words.

A simple way to move from letter recognition into word formation is with children's names—they are concrete, personal, and relevant to beginning readers. Most students already have a visual image of their name—they know what it looks like. By using something familiar, children are better able to see that words (e.g., their names) are made up of parts. They realize these parts are letters and sounds, that when combined, make words.

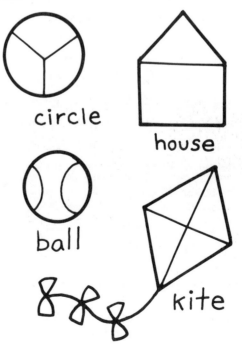

circle

house

ball

kite

bird

rainbow

An excellent way to explore letters and sounds in names is to use connecting paper dolls—each letter of a child's name is written on a separate doll to illustrate how letters connect to form words. Once children understand that sounds and sound patterns are combined to make words, extend learning by inviting children to cut apart and rearrange the "letter dolls," showing that some letter combinations make sense (letters *T, i, m* combine to form the name *Tim*), while others do not (letters *T, i, m* combined as *imT* have no meaning).

A useful tool for children as they learn to arrange letters into words is a "placement mat"—an index card or pre-cut sentence strip with a "start" dot on the left side. (You may choose to use a green dot to indicate starting position.) Because many children initially struggle with the left-to-right progression of English words, the dot can help guide them toward proper letter sequence.

It is extremely important to use the term *sounds*—the goal is for students to discover that sounds make up words. Refrain from saying the term *letters* or using letter names. When writing letters that correspond with sounds, use the sound symbols (graphemes—letter combinations that represent a phoneme) rather than the letters alone (e.g., /i/ to indicate the sound of *i* rather than the letter name).

Once students have thoroughly explored and discovered letters—connected sounds to individual letters, manipulated letters to form words, and recognized spelling patterns—they are ready to explore letter patterns in stories (e.g., vowel-variant storybooks). Students should be "overly exposed" to these letters and build inter-letter associations. For decoding to become an effortless process, students need extensive exposure to letter combinations and spelling patterns. Don't rush this step—if children consistently struggle or stop to decipher words, then spelling patterns have not been adequately learned and review is necessary. Children should extensively practice lower-level processes until they are automatic. Once this occurs, direct attention to higher-order processes of reading comprehension.

As children learn written language, continue to integrate phonemic-awareness activities into the regular reading program. Consistently practice and reinforce phonemic awareness—especially segmentation and manipulation—throughout the reading process. Proficient reading depends on the automatic ability to recognize frequently-used spelling patterns and translate them into sounds that form words. Studies show that differences in this ability are what separate good readers from poor readers. If students are phonologically proficient, they stand a much better chance of being good, strong, successful readers.

Dear Parents,

Did you know that children develop reading skills long before being introduced to written language? Playing with and practicing oral language helps children become better readers. In fact, phonemic awareness—the ability to differentiate and manipulate letter sounds—is critical to beginning reading development. Help your child become a better reader by practicing phonemic-awareness activities at home.

- Draw your child's attention to the sounds of his or her language with silly songs and poems. Include favorites such as *Down by the Bay* by Raffi, *If You're Happy and You Know It* by Nicki Weiss, *Sing Hey Diddle Diddle: 66 Nursery Rhymes with Their Traditional Tunes* by Beatrice Harrop, and *Six Sick Sheep: 101 Tongue Twisters* by Joanne Cole.

- Read and reread stories that play with language. Some excellent books include *There's a Wocket in My Pocket* by Dr. Seuss, *Silly Sally* by Audrey Wood, and *More Spaghetti, I Say!* by Rita Gelman.

- Have your child listen to and chant along with stories on tape. Make your own tape of songs and stories for your child to enjoy.

- Substitute and delete letters from common words to create your own silly sayings. For example, substitute *T* for *N* to change *Tommy eats tuna* to *Nommy eats nuna.* Celebrate Silly Word Day by speaking in rhyme or by greeting family members, replacing the first letter of their names with the letter of the day, such as *Faula* for *Paula.*

Dear Parents,

Before your child can learn to read, he or she needs to understand the connection between sounds and letters. Teaching your child to say and write the ABCs is not enough. Children need to hear and practice letter sounds as they see and write the symbols. Use the following activities to help your child associate sounds to written language.

- Have your child trace letters on multi-sensory surfaces such as cloth or sand. Ask him or her to say the corresponding sound as each letter is written.

- Construct letters using various materials such as macaroni, clay, or pipe cleaners. Have your child say the corresponding sounds as he or she feels each letter.

- Place magnetic letters on the refrigerator for your child to practice letter names and sounds, form words, and/or create messages.

- Have your child match letters to objects in and around the house. For example, place a plastic letter *B* on a bed, *T* on a table, and *F* by a flower.

- Draw your child's attention to letters and words in his or her environment, such as signs, cereal boxes, toy boxes, and menus.

Phonemic Awareness © 1997 Creative Teaching Press

Dear Parents,

As your child enters the wonderful world of reading, share in the enthusiasm and excitement by reading to him or her regularly. Your child will treasure these special times together, and you will be helping him or her become familiar with the sounds of the English language. Use the following tips as you read aloud and share favorite stories with your child.

- Select stories both you and your child will enjoy, such as those pertaining to a favorite hobby or sport. Include silly rhymes, chants, and tongue twisters for extra fun.

- Encourage your child to predict what comes next by looking at pictures or listening to word clues. For example, Jack and Jill went up the ____.

- Point out letter sounds in words as you read. Highlight words that have a specific phonetic sound, such as those that contain the /b/ sound. Have your child identify rhyming words aloud as you point to them in the story.

- Look for words with similar letter patterns (flow–er, pow–er). Have your child think of additional words with the same sound patterns.

- Dramatize your voice as you read. Your child will delight in hearing words "come to life." Take turns reading different parts, or invite your child to act out each role as you share stories aloud.

Dear Parents,

Parent involvement plays an important role in any child's academic success. You can help your child become a better reader by encouraging him or her to read to you regularly. Use the following simple techniques to guide and support your child's reading development.

- Select a specific time each night to read with your child—one that is free from interruptions. This will help your child understand and appreciate the importance of reading regularly.

- As your child reads aloud, give him or her sufficient time to "sound out" unfamiliar words. Offer hints and suggestions before saying the word. For example, looking at initial and final consonant sounds, trying short vowel sounds before using long ones, looking at other words in the sentence to see what makes sense.

- Be patient and supportive while your child reads. Allow time for him or her to self-correct and reread mispronounced words. Oftentimes, children will recognize mistakes as they continue to read the rest of the sentence.

- Break unfamiliar words into syllables so your child can focus on one syllable at a time. Use your hand or a paper strip to cover up extra syllables as your child sounds out each part.

- Point out and review phonetically-irregular words that do not follow conventional pronunciation, such as *two, was,* or *enough.* Have your child practice, memorize, and identify irregular words in context.

There was an old woman who lived in a shoe.

She had so many chi

Phonemic Awareness © 1997 Creative Teaching Press

Seeing Sounds

Task: sound matching

Materials
● hand-held mirrors

Directions

1. Distribute mirrors. Say words and have children repeat them as they look in the mirror. Point out teeth, tongue, and mouth positions as they say different letter sounds.

2. Divide the class into pairs. Have children hold mirrors for partners and say letter sounds again. Ask children to place their hands in front of their mouths as they speak, feeling the air expel.

3. Have children repeat the process a third time, saying the letters and placing their hands on their chins to feel mouth positions.

Phonemic Awareness © 1997 Creative Teaching Press

Nursery-Rhyme Rattle

Task: sound matching

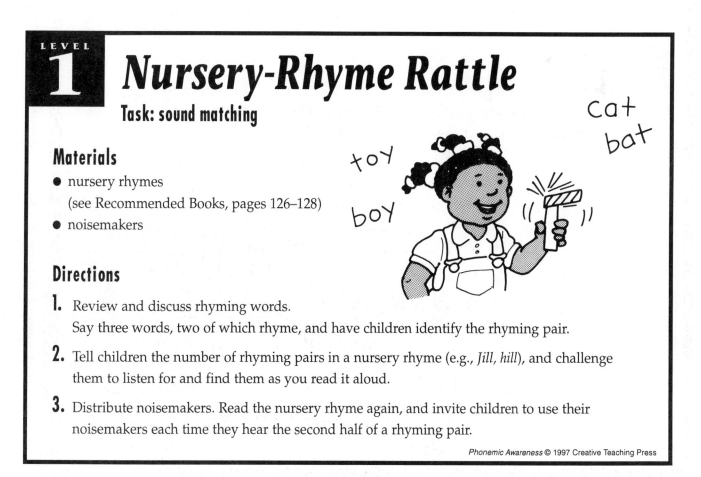

Materials
● nursery rhymes
  (see Recommended Books, pages 126–128)
● noisemakers

Directions

1. Review and discuss rhyming words.
Say three words, two of which rhyme, and have children identify the rhyming pair.

2. Tell children the number of rhyming pairs in a nursery rhyme (e.g., *Jill, hill*), and challenge them to listen for and find them as you read it aloud.

3. Distribute noisemakers. Read the nursery rhyme again, and invite children to use their noisemakers each time they hear the second half of a rhyming pair.

Phonemic Awareness © 1997 Creative Teaching Press

Getting to Know You

Task: sound matching

Materials

● none

Directions

1. Use this activity at the beginning of the year to help children learn classmates' names. Have children practice phoneme matching by asking a partner to name his or her favorite hobby or treat. Explain that "favorites" must begin with the same sound as the child's name. (e.g., *Patty* and *peanut butter*).

2. Invite children to introduce partners to the class, telling what he or she likes. For example, *Sam likes soccer and salamanders.*

3. Extend learning by having children draw pictures of their classmates on connecting paper dolls. Write each child's "favorite" on the bottom of his or her doll.

Phonemic Awareness © 1997 Creative Teaching Press

"Buggie" Boxes

Task: sound matching

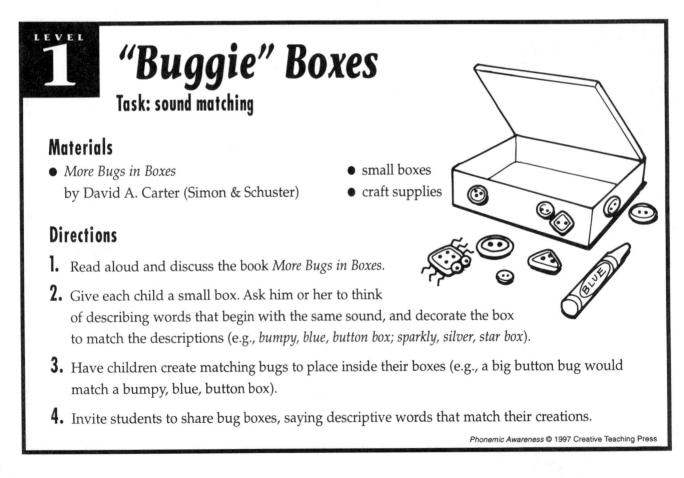

Materials

● *More Bugs in Boxes*
  by David A. Carter (Simon & Schuster)

● small boxes
● craft supplies

Directions

1. Read aloud and discuss the book *More Bugs in Boxes.*

2. Give each child a small box. Ask him or her to think of describing words that begin with the same sound, and decorate the box to match the descriptions (e.g., *bumpy, blue, button box; sparkly, silver, star box*).

3. Have children create matching bugs to place inside their boxes (e.g., a big button bug would match a bumpy, blue, button box).

4. Invite students to share bug boxes, saying descriptive words that match their creations.

Phonemic Awareness © 1997 Creative Teaching Press

Rhyme Time

Task: sound matching

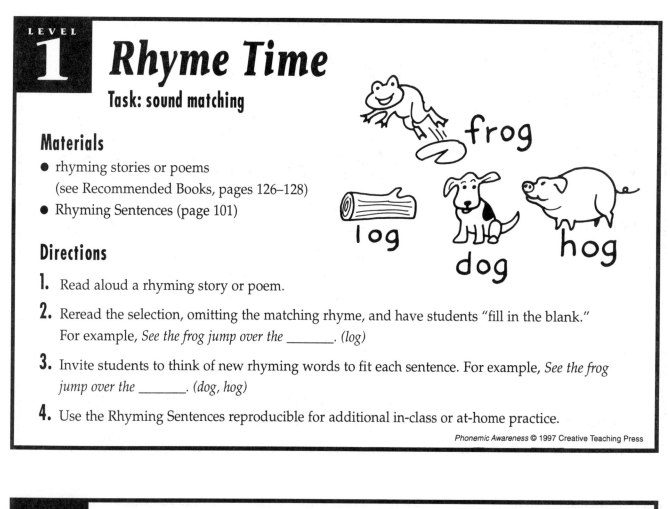

Materials

- rhyming stories or poems
  (see Recommended Books, pages 126–128)
- Rhyming Sentences (page 101)

Directions

1. Read aloud a rhyming story or poem.

2. Reread the selection, omitting the matching rhyme, and have students "fill in the blank." For example, *See the frog jump over the _____. (log)*

3. Invite students to think of new rhyming words to fit each sentence. For example, *See the frog jump over the _____. (dog, hog)*

4. Use the Rhyming Sentences reproducible for additional in-class or at-home practice.

Phonemic Awareness © 1997 Creative Teaching Press

What's My Sound?

Task: sound matching

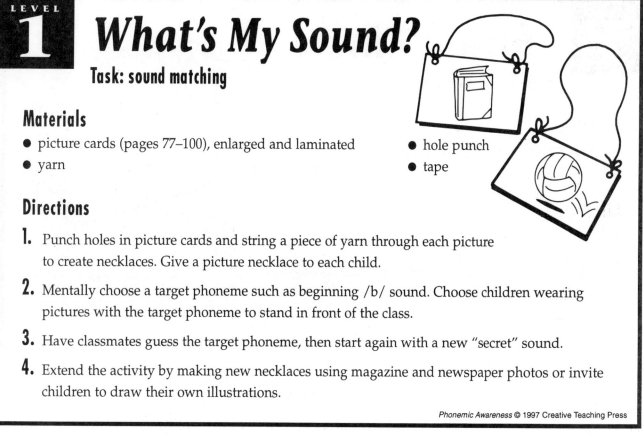

Materials

- picture cards (pages 77–100), enlarged and laminated
- yarn
- hole punch
- tape

Directions

1. Punch holes in picture cards and string a piece of yarn through each picture to create necklaces. Give a picture necklace to each child.

2. Mentally choose a target phoneme such as beginning /b/ sound. Choose children wearing pictures with the target phoneme to stand in front of the class.

3. Have classmates guess the target phoneme, then start again with a new "secret" sound.

4. Extend the activity by making new necklaces using magazine and newspaper photos or invite children to draw their own illustrations.

Phonemic Awareness © 1997 Creative Teaching Press

Rhyme Away

Task: sound matching

Materials
- Rhyme-Away stories (pages 102–104)
- colored chalk
- chalkboard eraser

Directions

1. In advance, draw simple pictures on the chalkboard similar to those shown on Rhyme-Away reproducibles. Tell children they are going to make the picture disappear by erasing it a little at a time—erasing parts that rhyme with words in the clues.

2. Read each rhyme of the Rhyme-Away stories aloud, omitting underlined words. Have children orally fill in the missing words, then invite volunteers to erase parts of the picture that correspond with the answers.

Phonemic Awareness © 1997 Creative Teaching Press

Draw a Rhyme

Task: sound matching

Materials
- Draw-a-Rhyme stories (pages 105–107)
- colored chalk
- paper
- crayons

Directions

1. Tell the class they are going to help you draw a monster. (This activity is the reverse of Rhyme Away—children use fill-in-the-blank clues to draw pictures.)

2. Read each rhyme of the Draw-a-Rhyme stories aloud, omitting underlined words. Have children orally fill in the missing words, then invite volunteers to draw the identified monster parts on the chalkboard to help complete the pictures.

3. As an alternative, invite children to draw their own pictures using paper and crayons as each clue is given.

Phonemic Awareness © 1997 Creative Teaching Press

No Zoo for You!

Task: sound matching

Materials
- animal picture cards (handmade or store bought)
- pocket chart

Directions

1. Place three animal cards in a pocket chart, including two that share a common phoneme (e.g., bear, bird, and goat).

2. Say each animal name together. Without offering any clues, invite a volunteer to remove the picture that does not belong (goat) and say, *No zoo for you!*

3. Repeat the same pattern with other picture cards, having children use deduction to determine which animals "enter the zoo" and which do not.

4. Repeat with new sound matches.

Phonemic Awareness © 1997 Creative Teaching Press

Silly Willy Song

Task: sound matching

Materials
- none

Directions

1. Teach the following verse to the tune of "Skip to My Lou." Invite children to sing along, completing the last line using words that rhyme with students' names.

Silly Willy, who should I choose? (repeat 3x)   *I choose* _____. *(Terri, berry)*

2. Continue the song, substituting new student names. Have everyone sing the main verse, and invite volunteers to say the new rhyming names.

3. As a variation, play a modified version of Duck, Duck, Goose while singing the song. Have the class sit in a circle and sing the first three lines while one child skips around the outside of the group. Ask the "skipper" to complete the last line, tapping the selected child on the shoulder and racing around the circle to sit in his or her spot.

Phonemic Awareness © 1997 Creative Teaching Press

Did You Ever?

Task: sound matching

Materials

- none

Directions

1. Teach children the following verse to the tune of "Have You Ever Seen a Lassie?"

   Did you ever see a cat, a cat, a cat,
   Did you ever see a cat sit on a rat?
   r–at, c–at,
   r–at, c–at,
   Did you ever see a cat sit on a rat?

2. Repeat the verse using other animal rhyming words.

3. For extra fun, invite children to use their names in the verse, singing both "sense" and "nonsense" rhymes *(Tony, pony; Susie, doosie).*

Oddball Out

Task: sound matching

Materials

- none

Directions

1. Ask children to listen carefully as you say three words. Explain that only two of the three words share a common sound. Have children identify the word that does not belong.

2. Say the words one at a time, then have children hold up one, two, or three fingers to indicate whether the first, second, or third word is the "oddball." Ask a volunteer to repeat the oddball word aloud.

3. As a variation, use pictures instead of words. Identify each picture aloud and have a volunteer choose the oddball picture.

Clap, Snap, or Tap?

Task: syllable counting

Materials

- multiple-syllable words or picture cards (pages 89–90)

Directions

1. Have a child say his or her first name and clap, snap, or tap the syllables as he or she speaks. Ask the rest of the class to silently count the number of claps, snaps, or taps, then repeat the hand motions while saying the child's name.

2. Continue the activity, inviting each child to choose whether to clap, snap, or tap the syllables in his or her name.

3. Extend the activity by having children clap, snap, or tap the number of syllables they hear in other multiple-syllable words such as *baseball, snowman,* and *under.* As a variation, invite students to tap different parts of their bodies, such as their stomachs or knees, as they repeat sounds in words.

Rhythm Time March

Task: syllable counting

Materials

- rhythm sticks, drums, or maracas (one per child)

Directions

1. Distribute instruments and ask children to sit in a circle.

2. Have students sing familiar songs with repetitive patterns ("Farmer in the Dell," "Twinkle Twinkle Little Star," "Old MacDonald"), tapping the syllabic beat in place of the repetitive words. For example, when singing "Farmer in the Dell," children tap the beat instead of singing the words, *High, ho, the derry-oh, the farmer in the dell.*

3. As a variation, have half the class tap the beat while others count the number of syllabic beats.

Rhyming Picture Sort

Task: sound matching

Materials
- Rhyming Picture Cards (pages 77–88)
- scissors

Directions

1. Copy a set of picture cards for yourself and each pair of children. Have volunteers identify and name each picture. Ask children to cut apart their cards and spread them out.

2. Hold up a picture card and ask children to select a rhyming picture from their set. Compare and discuss the different pictures selected, such as *ring* with *swing* or *wing*.

3. Extend the activity by having children sort picture cards by rhyming families. Invite partners to use picture cards to play a rhyme memory game.

Phonemic Awareness © 1997 Creative Teaching Press

Sing a Song of Sounds

Task: sound matching

If your name begins with /m/, stand up!

Materials
- picture cards (pages 77–100)

Directions

1. Have children sing the following song to the tune of "If You're Happy and You Know It."

   If your name begins with /m/, stand up,
   If your name begins with /m/, stand up,
   If your name begins with /m/, stand up and take a bow,
   If your name begins with /m/, stand up.

2. Repeat with different phonemes and movements such as clapping your hands, turning around, touching your toes, or jumping up and down.

3. As a variation, have children use picture cards with the song. For example, *If your picture begins with /s/, stand up.*

Phonemic Awareness © 1997 Creative Teaching Press

1 Silly Greetings

Task: sound matching

Materials
- student photographs

Directions

1. Collect or take student photographs.

2. Assign a letter to each day of the month (e.g., *T* for January 12th). Greet children by replacing the first letter of their names with the letter of the day, such as "Tally" for Sally.

3. Show student pictures one at a time and have the class greet their classmates with a "Good Morning" chant.

> *I say good morning to Tary (Mary),*
> *Good morning to Trew (Drew),*
> *Good morning to Tustin (Dustin) and Talice (Alice), too!*

Phonemic Awareness © 1997 Creative Teaching Press

---

1 Hink Pink

Task: sound matching

Materials
- none

Directions

1. Explain to children the definition of a hink pink—a pair of rhyming words that answers a riddle. Read aloud the following riddles, and invite children to guess the hink-pink answer.

> *What do you call a chubby kitty?* (fat cat)
> *What do you call a crying father?* (sad dad)
> *What do you call a desk that doesn't fall down?* (stable table)
> *What do you call a rabbit who tells jokes?* (funny bunny)

2. Invite children to think of other rhyming pairs. As a class, use these words to make clues for new hink pinks.

Phonemic Awareness © 1997 Creative Teaching Press

Who Did You Catch?

Tasks: syllable splitting, phoneme blending

Materials

● words from current classroom literature or General Words List (pages 70–73)

Directions

1. Practice blending onsets and rimes (e.g., *p–at* to form *pat, sw–ing* to form *swing*), then have children sing the following verse to the tune of "A-Hunting We Will Go."

> *A-searching we will go, a-searching we will go,*
> *We'll find a /h/ and add a /orse/,*
> *And now we have a horse!*

2. Repeat the verse using other onsets and rimes. To begin, use animal names (a more familiar context), then switch to word families such as *bat, hat,* and *mat.* For more advanced learning, segment the word into individual phonemes or transpose sound units. For example, *We'll catch an /at/ and add a /c/, and now we have a cat!*

Phonemic Awareness © 1997 Creative Teaching Press

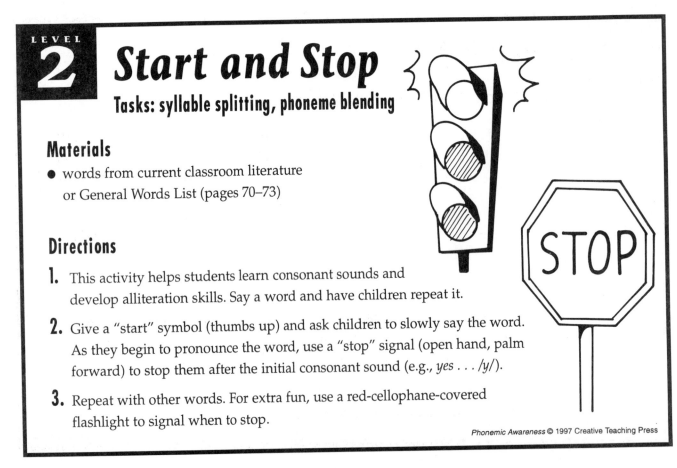

Start and Stop

Tasks: syllable splitting, phoneme blending

Materials

● words from current classroom literature or General Words List (pages 70–73)

Directions

1. This activity helps students learn consonant sounds and develop alliteration skills. Say a word and have children repeat it.

2. Give a "start" symbol (thumbs up) and ask children to slowly say the word. As they begin to pronounce the word, use a "stop" signal (open hand, palm forward) to stop them after the initial consonant sound (e.g., *yes . . . /y/*).

3. Repeat with other words. For extra fun, use a red-cellophane-covered flashlight to signal when to stop.

Phonemic Awareness © 1997 Creative Teaching Press

Punch It Out

Tasks: syllable splitting, phoneme blending

Materials

● none

/c/   /a/   /t/

Directions

1. Focus on target ending sounds by having children use hand motions as they say words. First, say the word *cat* without using hand motions.

2. Repeat the word and add hand motions. Slide your hand (palm down) from left to right as you say the word, then thrust a fist to "punch out" the last sound (/t/).

3. Have children repeat the word and hand motions. Repeat the activity with other words.

Phonemic Awareness © 1997 Creative Teaching Press

Break It in Half

Tasks: syllable splitting, phoneme blending

Materials

● two-syllable words from current classroom literature

cray-   -on

Directions

1. Say a two-syllable word and have children repeat it.

2. Model how to "break" the word in two using hand motions. Pantomime holding the word with two hands (e.g., two fists, side by side), then "breaking" it in half as you say the word. Say the first syllable (e.g., *des–* in the word *dessert*) as you move your right fist up and away from your left, then turn your right palm upward. Repeat with your left fist as you say the second syllable.

3. Have children practice hand motions with other two-syllable words.

Phonemic Awareness © 1997 Creative Teaching Press

Turtle Talk

Task: phoneme blending

T-u-r-t-l-e
T-a-l-k

Materials
- Turtle Talk (page 108)
- craft sticks
- crayons or markers
- glue
- words from current classroom literature or General Words List (pages 70–73)

Directions

1. This activity helps children "stretch out" words to hear how the phonemes blend together. Give a turtle picture to each child. Have him or her color and glue the turtle picture to a craft stick.

2. Explain to children that since turtles move very slowly and deliberately, they must also talk very s-l-o-w-l-y. Declare "Turtle Time" and say words slowly, one at a time, articulating each sound. Have children slowly move their "turtle sticks" from left to right as they repeat and "stretch out" each word.

Phonemic Awareness © 1997 Creative Teaching Press

Key to the Code

Task: phoneme blending

Materials
- keys (real or paper)
- paper cups

Directions

1. Tell children they are going to say words in "secret code," and the key to "unlocking" the code is to extend and blend the sounds together. Give an example: *If I say /h/ /a/ /m/, you say ham.* Practice several different words with the class, and invite volunteers to speak in "code" for their classmates.

2. Have students choose partners and give each pair a cup of ten keys. Ask one child from each pair to say words in "secret code." When a partner breaks the code for each word, he or she takes a key from the cup.

3. Have children continue until partners earn all ten keys, then invite students to switch roles.

Phonemic Awareness © 1997 Creative Teaching Press

Bubble-Gum Words

Task: phoneme blending

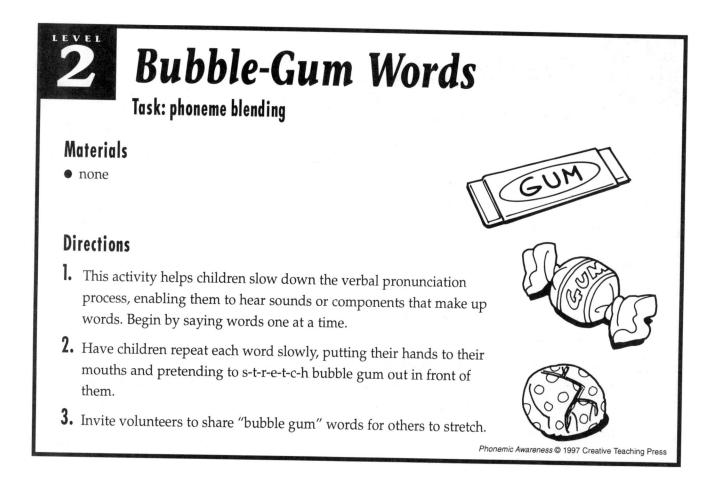

Materials

- none

Directions

1. This activity helps children slow down the verbal pronunciation process, enabling them to hear sounds or components that make up words. Begin by saying words one at a time.

2. Have children repeat each word slowly, putting their hands to their mouths and pretending to s-t-r-e-t-c-h bubble gum out in front of them.

3. Invite volunteers to share "bubble gum" words for others to stretch.

Phonemic Awareness © 1997 Creative Teaching Press

Name Chant

Task: phoneme blending

Materials

- class list

Directions

1. Say the following chant to children:

   *It begins with /t/,
   And it ends with /im/.
   Put them together,
   And they say _____. (Tim)*

2. Have children blend the sounds together and chorus the correct answer.

3. Repeat the chant using each student's name. Invite children to stand and bow when their names are spoken.

Phonemic Awareness © 1997 Creative Teaching Press

The Sounds in the Word

Task: phoneme blending

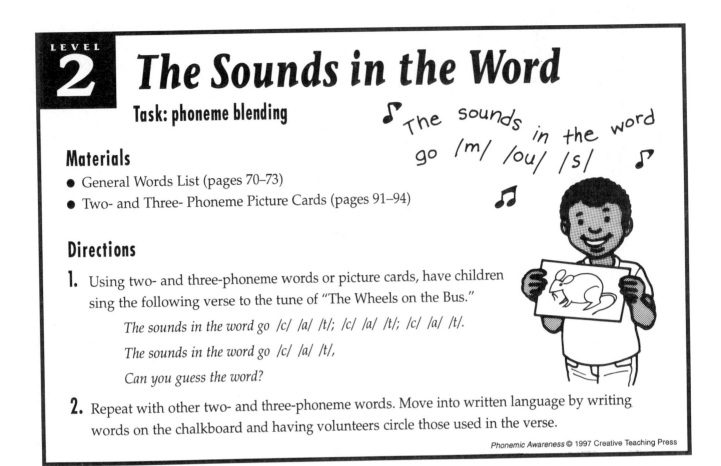

The sounds in the word
go /m/ /ou/ /s/

Materials

- General Words List (pages 70–73)
- Two- and Three- Phoneme Picture Cards (pages 91–94)

Directions

1. Using two- and three-phoneme words or picture cards, have children sing the following verse to the tune of "The Wheels on the Bus."

   The sounds in the word go /c/ /a/ /t/; /c/ /a/ /t/; /c/ /a/ /t/.

   The sounds in the word go /c/ /a/ /t/,

   Can you guess the word?

2. Repeat with other two- and three-phoneme words. Move into written language by writing words on the chalkboard and having volunteers circle those used in the verse.

Phonemic Awareness © 1997 Creative Teaching Press

Patty-Cake Sounds

Task: phoneme blending

c-at p-in f-un

Materials

- words from current classroom literature or General Words List (pages 70–73)

Directions

1. Ask children to sit in a circle. Show them how to pat their legs and clap in a 2:1 rhythm (two pats on the legs, then one hand clap).

2. Have them repeat onsets and rhymes, such as *c–at* or *p–in*, while patting and clapping the beat. For example, /c/ /at/ cat (pat, pat, clap).

3. Extend learning by using instruments to keep the beat while blending onsets and rimes.

Phonemic Awareness © 1997 Creative Teaching Press

Talking Ghost

Task: phoneme blending

Materials

- white construction paper
- scissors
- crayons or markers

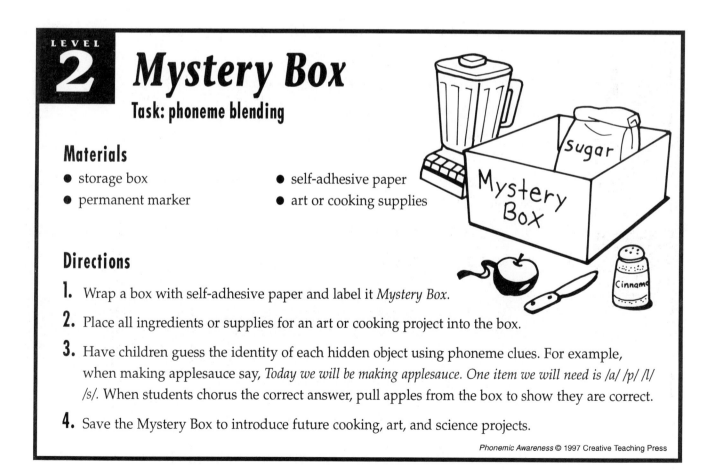

Directions

1. Have each child draw and cut out a picture of a ghost.

2. Say a segmented word, then have children "hold onto the sounds" as they blend them together aloud. Tell them to speak like ghosts, extending the sounds of words into a slow, drawn-out wail. For example, you say /h/ /ou/ /s/, and they say, *hhhooouuusssseee*.

3. Invite children to move their ghosts as they say the sounds. Repeat with other words.

Phonemic Awareness © 1997 Creative Teaching Press

LEVEL 2 Mystery Box

Task: phoneme blending

Materials

- storage box
- permanent marker
- self-adhesive paper
- art or cooking supplies

Directions

1. Wrap a box with self-adhesive paper and label it *Mystery Box*.

2. Place all ingredients or supplies for an art or cooking project into the box.

3. Have children guess the identity of each hidden object using phoneme clues. For example, when making applesauce say, *Today we will be making applesauce. One item we will need is /a/ /p/ /l/ /s/.* When students chorus the correct answer, pull apples from the box to show they are correct.

4. Save the Mystery Box to introduce future cooking, art, and science projects.

Phonemic Awareness © 1997 Creative Teaching Press

Pop-Up People
Task: phoneme blending

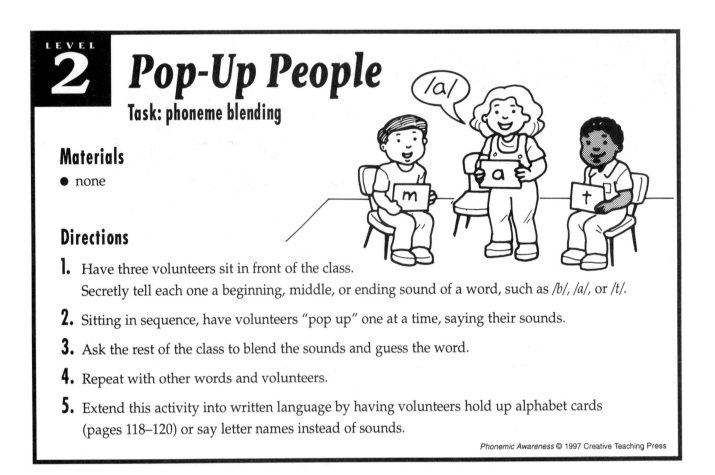

Materials
● none

Directions

1. Have three volunteers sit in front of the class.
   Secretly tell each one a beginning, middle, or ending sound of a word, such as /b/, /a/, or /t/.

2. Sitting in sequence, have volunteers "pop up" one at a time, saying their sounds.

3. Ask the rest of the class to blend the sounds and guess the word.

4. Repeat with other words and volunteers.

5. Extend this activity into written language by having volunteers hold up alphabet cards
   (pages 118–120) or say letter names instead of sounds.

Phonemic Awareness © 1997 Creative Teaching Press

Sound Bingo
Tasks: phoneme isolation, sound matching

Materials
● Bingo Game Card (page 110) and Sound Cards (page 111)
● Bingo Record Sheet (page 109), laminated for reuse
● counters
● scissors, glue

Directions

1. Have children make their own bingo cards by cutting and pasting Sound Cards to the Bingo Game Card in random order.

2. Begin each game by telling children whether to listen for beginning, middle, or ending sounds. Explain how to play Sound Bingo—children listen to each word, then use a counter to cover the bingo space with the matching sound.

3. Use the Bingo Record Sheet to keep track of words you say for each sound. Tell children to call out *Bingo!* when they have covered a row, then read the sounds while you check your sheet.

Phonemic Awareness © 1997 Creative Teaching Press

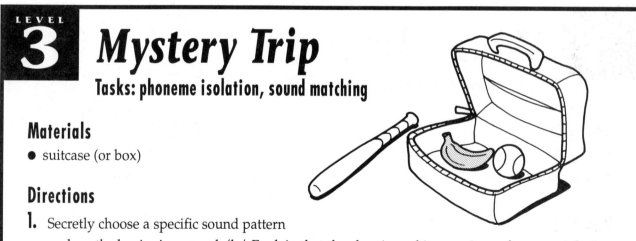

LEVEL 3 — Web of Sounds

Tasks: phoneme isolation, sound matching

Materials
- craft supplies (black construction paper, black pipe cleaners, wiggly eyes, glue, tape, white crayon)
- yarn balls (one per group)

Directions

1. In advance, use craft supplies to make "phoneme spiders." Use a white crayon to write different ending phonemes (e.g., /at/, /og/, or /ick/) on each spider body.

2. Take children outdoors and have small groups stand in large circles. Place a spider in the center of each circle, and have a child from each group say a word ending with the "spider sound." He or she then tosses a yarn ball to another player while still holding onto one end. The child catching the ball must then think of another word. Children "weave the web" until they run out of words. Continue the game by having groups exchange phoneme spiders.

Phonemic Awareness © 1997 Creative Teaching Press

LEVEL 3 — Mystery Trip

Tasks: phoneme isolation, sound matching

Materials
- suitcase (or box)

Directions

1. Secretly choose a specific sound pattern such as the beginning sound /b/. Explain that the class is packing a suitcase for a special trip, and only the items that have the "secret sound" in their names will fit in the suitcase.

2. Pretend to place objects in the suitcase, all of which fit the secret sound pattern, such as *bunny* or *ball.* Invite children who think they know the pattern to "pack" an object, saying the name aloud. Ask them to keep the identity of the sound a secret. Tell children whether or not their objects fit (i.e., contain the secret sound).

3. Continue playing until several children figure out the pattern, then tell them the secret sound. Play again using other secret sounds.

Phonemic Awareness © 1997 Creative Teaching Press

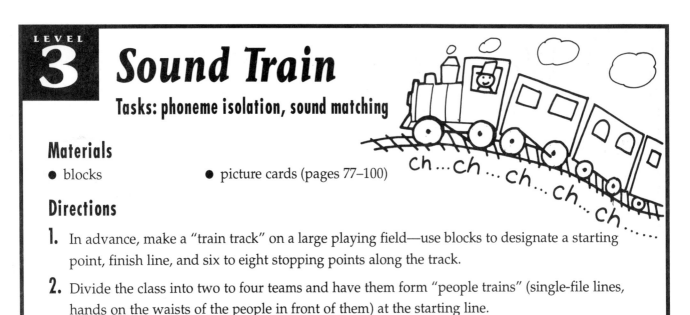

LEVEL 3

Sound Train

Tasks: phoneme isolation, sound matching

Materials

- blocks
- picture cards (pages 77–100)

Directions

1. In advance, make a "train track" on a large playing field—use blocks to designate a starting point, finish line, and six to eight stopping points along the track.

2. Divide the class into two to four teams and have them form "people trains" (single-file lines, hands on the waists of the people in front of them) at the starting line.

3. Hold up two pictures, say the names, and have children identify the common sound. The first team to do so moves up the track to the first stopping point, making a "choo choo" sound to match the identified phoneme. For example, if the target sound is /d/, they move up the track saying /d/ /d/ /d/ . . .). Continue the game with other pictures. The first train to reach the finish line wins.

Phonemic Awareness © 1997 Creative Teaching Press

LEVEL 3

Sound Dominos

Tasks: phoneme isolation, sound matching

Materials

- Sound Dominos (page 112) or magazine cutouts
- craft sticks
- scissors, glue

Directions

1. Have partners cut and paste small pictures to both ends of craft sticks to make 15 to 20 picture dominos. Have each child choose four dominos and place the rest face down in a pile.

2. Explain that the object of the game is to get rid of your dominos by matching picture sounds. Have one player from each pair place a domino on a tabletop or the floor. The other player must then match one picture on that domino with one of their own. (For example, cat and car pictures match because they both begin with /c/.) If partners have no match, have them choose from the pile until one is found.

3. Partners take turns adding dominos to the pattern. A player wins when he or she runs out of dominos. (If all extra dominos are used, the player with the fewest unmatched dominos wins.)

Phonemic Awareness © 1997 Creative Teaching Press

What Big Ears You Have!

Task: phoneme isolation

Materials
- Mickey Mouse hat (or paper elephant ears)

Directions

1. Use Mickey Mouse ears to emphasize the importance of listening to sounds. Say the following verse with children. Choose a child to wear the Mickey Mouse ears and identify the sound (/d/).

> Children: *Listen, listen, loud and clear*
> *What's the first sound that you hear?*
> Teacher: *Doggie, dolly, dark, and daddy*
> Children: *Tell me, tell me, what you hear.*

2. Repeat with new word patterns. Modify the verse to identify middle and ending sounds (e.g., *What's the last sound that you hear?*).

Phonemic Awareness © 1997 Creative Teaching Press

Puppet Pop-Ups

Task: phoneme isolation

Materials
- old, solid-colored socks
- craft supplies (yarn, wiggly eyes, felt, rubber bands, scissors, glue)

Directions

1. Ask children to make sock puppets using craft items, scissors, and glue. Have children put their hands inside sock puppets, then place rubber bands around their hands to create mouths for their puppets to "speak" the target sound.

2. Ask children to sit on the floor in a semi-circle, wearing sock puppets on their hands. Have them keep puppets "hidden" in their laps. Say a target word, then invite children to "pop up" their puppets each time they hear you call out a word with the same beginning sound. For example, if the target word is *pencil* and you call out *pot*, children raise their puppets—if you call out *red*, they keep their puppets hidden.

Phonemic Awareness © 1997 Creative Teaching Press

Where's That Sound?

Task: phoneme isolation

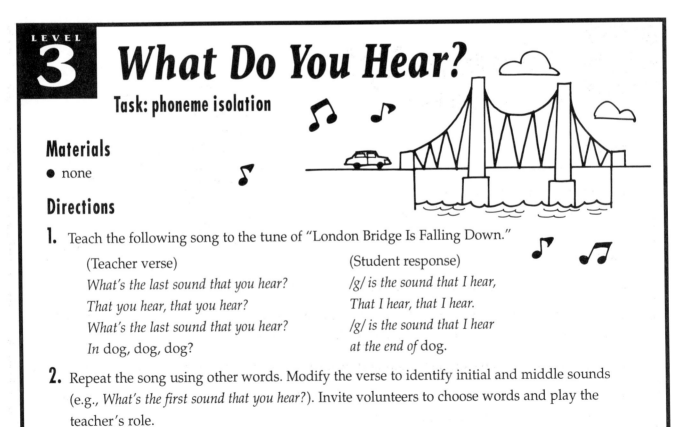

Materials

- Puppet Patterns (page 113)
- tagboard
- glue
- craft sticks (two per child)
- words from current classroom literature or General Words List (pages 70–73)

Directions

1. Glue puppet patterns on tagboard, and have each student choose a puppet to color, cut out, and glue to a craft stick.

2. Say a target sound (e.g., /b/). Read three-phoneme words and have children use extra craft sticks to point to the front, middle, or end of their puppets to indicate whether the target sound is heard at the beginning, middle, or end of the words.

Phonemic Awareness © 1997 Creative Teaching Press

What Do You Hear?

Task: phoneme isolation

Materials

- none

Directions

1. Teach the following song to the tune of "London Bridge Is Falling Down."

   (Teacher verse)
   What's the last sound that you hear?
   That you hear, that you hear?
   What's the last sound that you hear?
   In dog, dog, dog?

   (Student response)
   /g/ is the sound that I hear,
   That I hear, that I hear.
   /g/ is the sound that I hear
   at the end of dog.

2. Repeat the song using other words. Modify the verse to identify initial and middle sounds (e.g., *What's the first sound that you hear?*). Invite volunteers to choose words and play the teacher's role.

Phonemic Awareness © 1997 Creative Teaching Press

3 *What Is It?*

Task: phoneme isolation

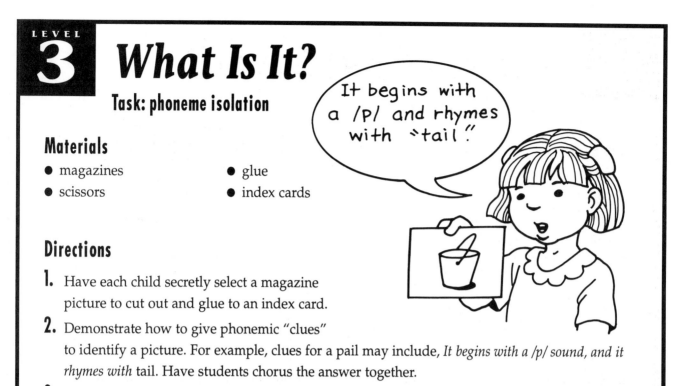

It begins with a /p/ and rhymes with "tail."

Materials

- magazines
- scissors
- glue
- index cards

Directions

1. Have each child secretly select a magazine picture to cut out and glue to an index card.

2. Demonstrate how to give phonemic "clues" to identify a picture. For example, clues for a pail may include, *It begins with a /p/ sound, and it rhymes with* tail. Have students chorus the answer together.

3. Have children take turns giving phonemic clues for their pictures. Offer assistance when needed, or invite children to work with partners.

Phonemic Awareness © 1997 Creative Teaching Press

---

3 *Thumbs Up!*

Task: phoneme isolation

Materials

- smiley stickers
- words from current classroom literature or General Words List (pages 70–73)

Directions

1. Give a smiley sticker to each child to stick on his or her thumb.

2. Select a target sound such as /d/. Instruct children to give a "smiley thumbs up" signal each time they hear the target sound at the beginning of a word.

3. Read words from the word list, inviting students to indicate which ones contain the target sound.

4. Change the target sound and repeat the activity with other words. After practice with initial sounds, have children signal middle or ending sounds.

Phonemic Awareness © 1997 Creative Teaching Press

Give It the Test

Task: phoneme isolation

Materials

- bag of objects beginning with the same sound (nut, nickel, napkin)

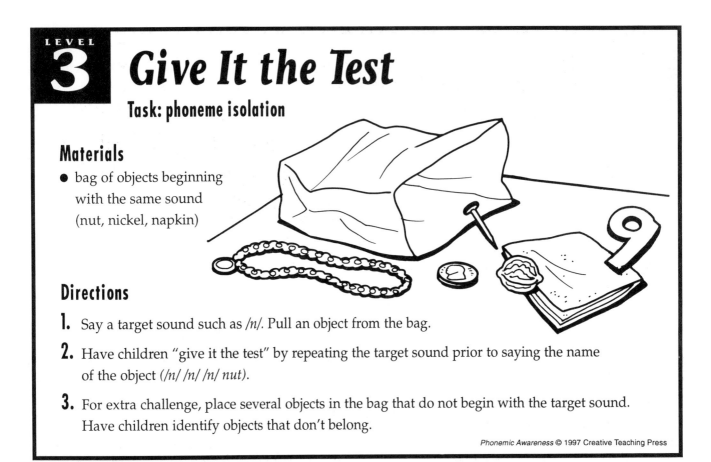

Directions

1. Say a target sound such as /n/. Pull an object from the bag.

2. Have children "give it the test" by repeating the target sound prior to saying the name of the object (/n/ /n/ /n/ nut).

3. For extra challenge, place several objects in the bag that do not begin with the target sound. Have children identify objects that don't belong.

Phonemic Awareness © 1997 Creative Teaching Press

Three in a Row

Task: phoneme isolation

Materials

- Rhyming Picture Cards (pages 77–88)

Directions

1. Have children choose partners and give each pair a set of picture cards. The object of the game is to be the first player to place three rhyming picture cards in a row.

2. Have children shuffle the cards and distribute four to each player. Ask each child to choose one "target" picture to start his or her row.

3. Have players take turns selecting cards from their pile. At each turn, if a child selects (or holds in his or her hand) a card that rhymes with the target picture, he or she places it in the row. If the card does not match, it is placed in the "discard" pile. Only one rhyming card can be placed per turn. The game ends when a player has three rhyming pictures in a row.

Phonemic Awareness © 1997 Creative Teaching Press

LEVEL 3

Bag of Sounds

Task: phoneme isolation

Materials

- small objects
- large bag
- trays

Directions

1. Collect pairs of objects that have the same beginning sounds, such as book and ball, pencil and penny, and bead and banana. Place one object from each pair in a bag and the other on a tray.

2. Working with a small group, have children pull objects from the bag and find matching objects on the tray.

3. Expand the activity by inviting children to find small, matching objects in the classroom to add to the tray and bag.

Phonemic Awareness © 1997 Creative Teaching Press

LEVEL 3

Scavenger Hunt

Task: phoneme isolation

Materials

- six large paper bags
- marker
- objects whose names begin with sounds /t/, /l/, /r/, /k/, /n/, and /d/
- pictures of objects with the same ending sounds (optional)

Directions

1. In advance, write a beginning sound on each bag. (If children are nonreaders, staple pictures with the target sound on the bags.) Place objects matching the sounds around the classroom.

2. Divide the class into six teams and give each team a "sound bag." Have groups find small classroom objects whose beginning sounds match those on the bags. Ask children to place the objects in their bags.

3. Have children gather in a circle after five minutes to share their results. Extend learning by having children re-hide objects from their bags, then switch bags with classmates and search for objects with matching *ending* sounds.

Phonemic Awareness © 1997 Creative Teaching Press

Grab Bag

Task: phoneme isolation

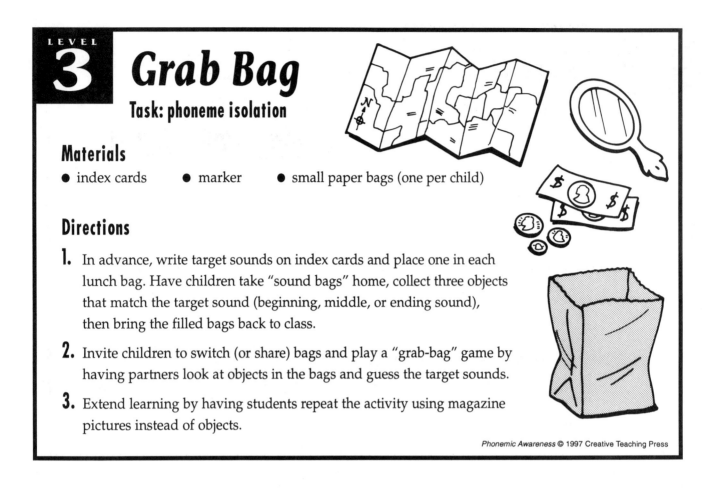

Materials

- index cards
- marker
- small paper bags (one per child)

Directions

1. In advance, write target sounds on index cards and place one in each lunch bag. Have children take "sound bags" home, collect three objects that match the target sound (beginning, middle, or ending sound), then bring the filled bags back to class.

2. Invite children to switch (or share) bags and play a "grab-bag" game by having partners look at objects in the bags and guess the target sounds.

3. Extend learning by having students repeat the activity using magazine pictures instead of objects.

Phonemic Awareness © 1997 Creative Teaching Press

Catch the Sound

Task: phoneme isolation

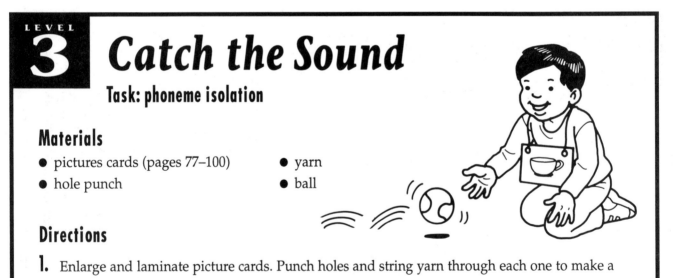

Materials

- pictures cards (pages 77–100)
- hole punch
- yarn
- ball

Directions

1. Enlarge and laminate picture cards. Punch holes and string yarn through each one to make a necklace. Distribute picture necklaces and have children wear them while sitting in a circle.

2. Designate a target sound (e.g., ending sound /t/). Give one child a ball, and have him or her roll it to a classmate wearing a picture that fits the pattern (e.g., cat). Ask the second child to roll it to a third, and so on.

3. Challenge children to keep the ball in constant motion as you change the target sound, such as from ending sound /t/ to beginning sound /m/.

Phonemic Awareness © 1997 Creative Teaching Press

Listen Up!

Task: phoneme isolation

Materials

- list of words containing target sound
- overhead marker, transparency, and projector
- graph paper
- crayons

Directions

1. In advance, generate a list of words containing a target sound. For example, words for the target sound /t/ could include *cat, tap,* and *stop.* Use graph paper to make bar graphs, labeling three columns *B, M,* and *E.* Make photocopies for children and a transparency to use for instruction.

2. Have children listen for the target sound in words you say aloud, then color a space on their graph paper to indicate whether it is heard at the beginning *(B),* middle *(M),* or end *(E)* of the word. Show examples using the overhead transparency before having children work independently.

Phonemic Awareness © 1997 Creative Teaching Press

Picture Spelling

Task: phoneme isolation

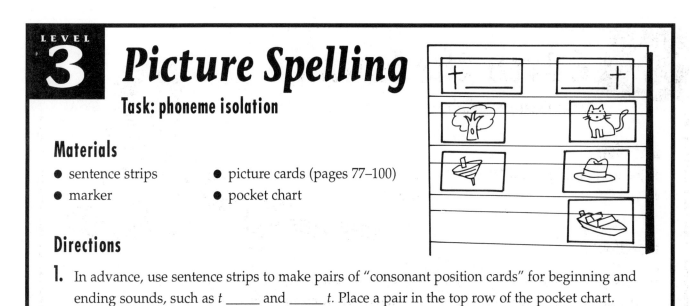

Materials

- sentence strips
- marker
- picture cards (pages 77–100)
- pocket chart

Directions

1. In advance, use sentence strips to make pairs of "consonant position cards" for beginning and ending sounds, such as *t* _____ and _____ *t.* Place a pair in the top row of the pocket chart.

2. Show a picture card to children and have them decide whether it contains the designated consonant sound at the beginning or end of the word. Invite a volunteer to place the picture under the appropriate consonant card.

3. Continue with other pictures, then exchange consonant position cards and repeat with a new target sound.

Phonemic Awareness © 1997 Creative Teaching Press

Color-Coded Sounds

Task: phoneme isolation

Materials

- index cards
- pencil
- crayons
- counters

Directions

1. In advance, draw three horizontal fill-in-the-blank lines on each index card to designate beginning, middle, and ending sound positions of a word. Give a card to each child and have him or her color the first line green, the middle line blue, and the last line red.

2. Designate a target sound. Ask children to listen to a word containing the target sound, then place a counter on the index card to indicate where they hear the sound—on the green line if it's a beginning sound, the blue line if it's a middle sound, or the red line if it's an ending sound. Repeat with other words.

Phonemic Awareness © 1997 Creative Teaching Press

Penny Push

Task: phoneme isolation

Materials

- index cards
- pennies
- permanent marker
- phoneme picture cards (pages 91–100)

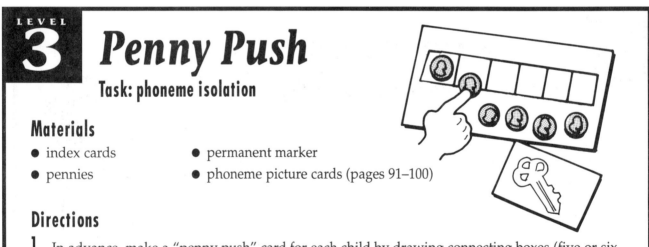

Directions

1. In advance, make a "penny push" card for each child by drawing connecting boxes (five or six squares attached side by side) on individual index cards. Give each child a card and have him or her place a penny underneath each blank box.

2. Identify a picture, then demonstrate how to slide a penny into a box for each phoneme heard. (e.g., for a picture of a key, slide a penny into the first box as you slowly say, /k/, and another penny into the second box as you say, /ey/.)

3. Have children practice with several pictures. Increase the difficulty by using four- and five-phoneme picture cards.

Phonemic Awareness © 1997 Creative Teaching Press

4 *I Spy*

Tasks: phoneme counting, phoneme isolation

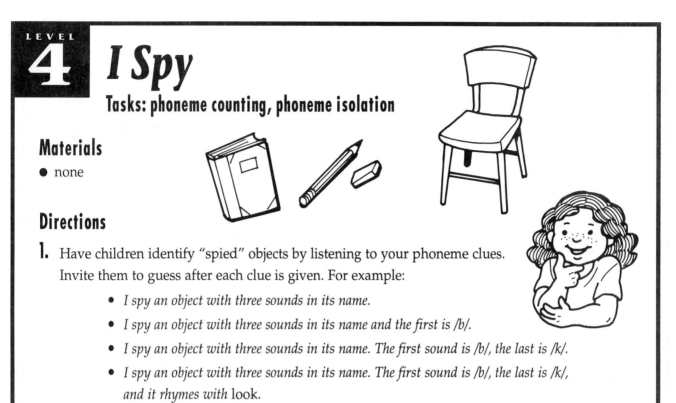

Materials

● none

Directions

1. Have children identify "spied" objects by listening to your phoneme clues. Invite them to guess after each clue is given. For example:

- *I spy an object with three sounds in its name.*
- *I spy an object with three sounds in its name and the first is /b/.*
- *I spy an object with three sounds in its name. The first sound is /b/, the last is /k/.*
- *I spy an object with three sounds in its name. The first sound is /b/, the last is /k/, and it rhymes with* look.

2. Repeat with different objects. Invite volunteers to provide "I Spy" clues for their classmates.

Phonemic Awareness © 1997 Creative Teaching Press

---

4 *Tap and Sweep*

Tasks: phoneme counting, phoneme blending

Materials

● words from current classroom literature or General Words List (pages 70–73)

Directions

1. Say single-syllable words one at a time. Have children "knock" on tabletops as they say each phoneme, moving their hands from left to right to show whether the sound comes at the beginning, middle, or end of the word.

2. Have children go back to the first tap position and sweep their fists on the table from left to right, "blending" the sounds together—ask children to say the word as they show the hand motion.

3. As an alternative, have children extend fingers to count off each phoneme, then use a sweeping-hand motion as they blend the sounds together.

Phonemic Awareness © 1997 Creative Teaching Press

LEVEL 4

Count the Sounds

Task: phoneme counting

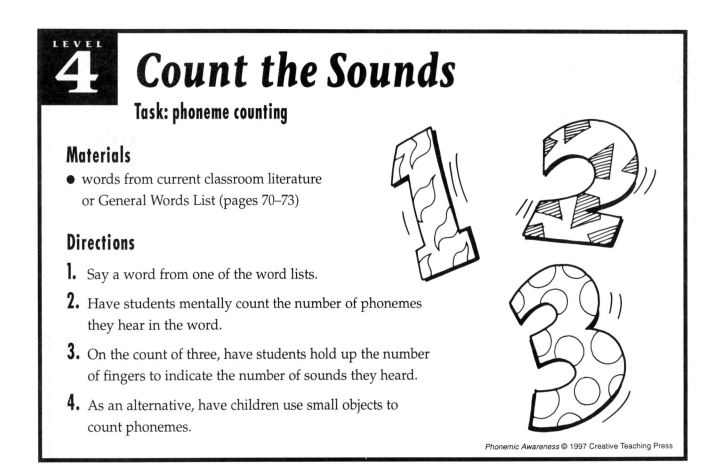

Materials

- words from current classroom literature or General Words List (pages 70–73)

Directions

1. Say a word from one of the word lists.

2. Have students mentally count the number of phonemes they hear in the word.

3. On the count of three, have students hold up the number of fingers to indicate the number of sounds they heard.

4. As an alternative, have children use small objects to count phonemes.

Phonemic Awareness © 1997 Creative Teaching Press

LEVEL 4

Classifying Objects

Task: phoneme counting

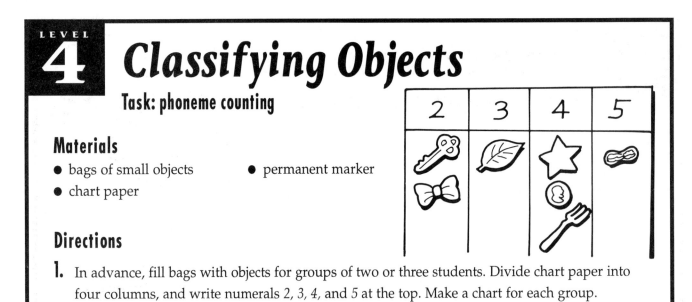

Materials

- bags of small objects
- chart paper
- permanent marker

Directions

1. In advance, fill bags with objects for groups of two or three students. Divide chart paper into four columns, and write numerals *2, 3, 4,* and *5* at the top. Make a chart for each group.

2. Have children from each group pull an object from the bag and count the number of phonemes they hear in the object's name. Ask them to place the object under the correct column on the graph. For example, a key would be placed under the *2* column; a penny would be placed under the *4* column.

3. Have students continue until their bags are empty. Invite students to share their results.

Phonemic Awareness © 1997 Creative Teaching Press

Sound Baseball

Task: phoneme counting

Materials
- items to make baseball field (poster board, markers, velcro)
- items to make baseball cards (pictures, index cards, labels)
- baseball mitt (real or paper)
- construction paper, scissors, glue

Directions

1. In advance, draw a baseball diamond on poster board and stick Velcro on each base. Prepare game cards by cutting and gluing pictures onto baseball-shaped index cards. Make team markers by sticking Velcro to laminated paper baseball caps.

2. Place game cards in a baseball mitt in front of the class. Divide the class into two teams and "pitch" laminated baseballs to each player.

3. Have teams score "hits" or "outs" by correctly or incorrectly identifying the number of sounds illustrated on a game card (e.g., two for a picture of a key). Attach team baseball caps to the bases to show progress, and write scores on the chalkboard.

Phonemic Awareness © 1997 Creative Teaching Press

Jump to the Sounds

Tasks: phoneme segmentation, phoneme counting

Materials
- jump ropes (one per child)
- picture cards (pages 77–100)

Directions

1. Give each child a jump rope.

2. Show a picture of an object. Ask children to say the phonemes that comprise the object's name.

3. Using jump ropes, have children jump for each phoneme of the word. For example, children would jump three times for the word *cat*—/c/ /a/ /t/.

4. Repeat using other picture cards or classroom objects. (Note: For children who can't jump rope, have them jump over a stationary, lowered rope.)

Phonemic Awareness © 1997 Creative Teaching Press

Tap to the Sounds

Tasks: phoneme segmentation, phoneme counting

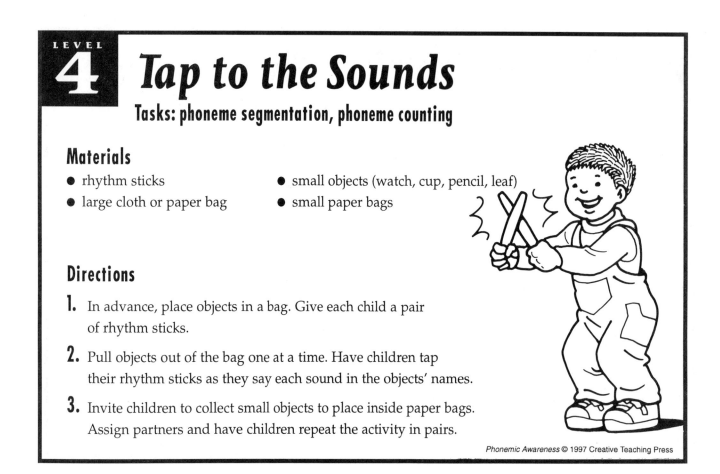

Materials

- rhythm sticks
- large cloth or paper bag
- small objects (watch, cup, pencil, leaf)
- small paper bags

Directions

1. In advance, place objects in a bag. Give each child a pair of rhythm sticks.

2. Pull objects out of the bag one at a time. Have children tap their rhythm sticks as they say each sound in the objects' names.

3. Invite children to collect small objects to place inside paper bags. Assign partners and have children repeat the activity in pairs.

Phonemic Awareness © 1997 Creative Teaching Press

Eat Your Words

Tasks: phoneme segmentation, phoneme counting, phoneme blending

Materials

- paper towels
- fish crackers, raisins, or small candies (12–20 per child)
- words from current classroom literature

Directions

1. Say a word containing two or three sounds. Have children move food pieces to form a horizontal line, one for each sound they hear in the word. Ask them to say the phonemes as they move the food pieces to the line.

2. Have each child "sweep" his or her finger under the food line and blend the sounds together to say the word.

3. Repeat the word slowly as children eat the food piece representing each sound. Continue the activity with new words until all food is eaten.

Phonemic Awareness © 1997 Creative Teaching Press

LEVEL 4
Put It Together, Take It Apart

Tasks: phoneme segmentation, phoneme counting, phoneme blending

Materials
● linking cubes

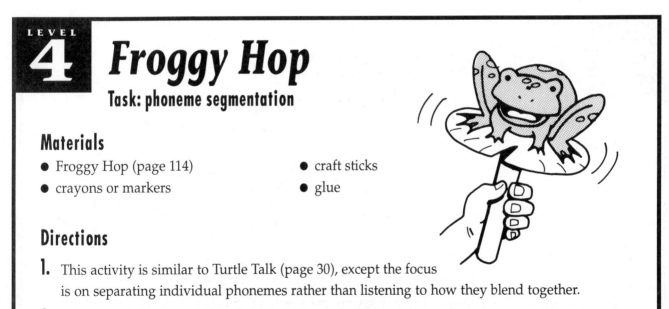

/c/ /u/ /p/ ... cup!

Directions

1. Distribute several linking cubes to each child.

2. Say a simple word such as *duck.* Have children repeat the word slowly, taking a cube for each sound they hear and linking cubes together.

3. Ask children to touch each linked cube from left to right, saying the corresponding sounds with each movement. Have them sweep their hand across the cubes as they blend the sounds to form the word.

4. Have children take the linking cubes apart, "breaking" the word as they say the corresponding phonemes for the last time. Repeat with other words.

Phonemic Awareness © 1997 Creative Teaching Press

LEVEL 4
Froggy Hop

Task: phoneme segmentation

Materials
● Froggy Hop (page 114)
● crayons or markers
● craft sticks
● glue

Directions

1. This activity is similar to Turtle Talk (page 30), except the focus is on separating individual phonemes rather than listening to how they blend together.

2. Give a frog picture to each child. Have him or her color and glue the frog to a craft stick.

3. Explain how frogs jump from rock to rock as they travel. Declare "Froggy Fun Time." Have children use their "frog sticks" as they sequentially separate different phonemes of a word, pausing between sounds. For example, children move frog sticks three hops to the right as they say the segmented word /h/ /a/ /t/.

Phonemic Awareness © 1997 Creative Teaching Press

Echoes

Tasks: phoneme segmentation, phoneme blending

Materials

● none

Directions

1. Teach children about echoes and how they work.

2. Invite children to sit under their desks and pretend to be echoes.
Say a segmented word aloud and have children echo the blended word in response.
For example, say, /p/ /a/ /n/, and have children say the word *pan.*

3. After sufficient practice, divide the class into two groups and have them sit at opposite sides
of the classroom. Have one group say a segmented word and the other group echo the blended
word in response.

Phonemic Awareness © 1997 Creative Teaching Press

Begin with Green

Tasks: phoneme segmentation, phoneme blending

Materials

● green, yellow, and red linking cubes
● words from current classroom literature
or General Words List (pages 70–73)

Directions

1. Give each child one green and one red cube linked together.
Ask students to lay the cubes horizontally, with the green cube to the left.

2. Read aloud two-phoneme words one at a time. Have children point to the green cube while
saying the first phoneme in the word and the red cube for the second. Then ask them to move
their finger across the cubes from left to right as they blend the sounds to say the word.

3. When children succeed with two-phoneme words, have them add a yellow cube between the
green and red cubes and repeat the task with three-phoneme words.

Phonemic Awareness © 1997 Creative Teaching Press

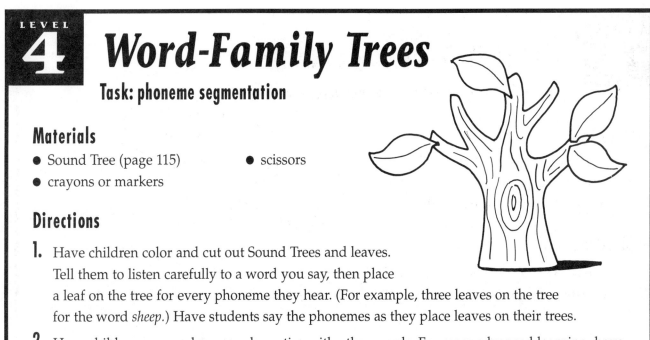

Head, Waist, Toes

Tasks: phoneme segmentation, phoneme isolation

Materials

- words from current classroom literature or General Words List (pages 70–73)

Directions

1. Have children stand as they listen to you say a three-phoneme word.

2. Say each phoneme of the word separately and ask children to place their hands on their heads, waists, or toes to indicate whether the sound is at the beginning, middle, or end of the word. Have students repeat the sounds as they take positions.

3. Repeat with additional three-phoneme words. For variation, say phonemes faster and faster as the game progresses. Extend the activity to four-phoneme words using head, waist, knees, and toes as the four body positions.

4. Send word lists home and invite children to play the game with their parents.

Phonemic Awareness © 1997 Creative Teaching Press

Word-Family Trees

Task: phoneme segmentation

Materials

- Sound Tree (page 115)
- crayons or markers
- scissors

Directions

1. Have children color and cut out Sound Trees and leaves. Tell them to listen carefully to a word you say, then place a leaf on the tree for every phoneme they hear. (For example, three leaves on the tree for the word *sheep*.) Have students say the phonemes as they place leaves on their trees.

2. Have children remove leaves and practice with other words. For more advanced learning, have children color-code leaves to show word families. For example, place one blue leaf and two red leaves on the tree for the word *bat*, then exchange the blue leaf for a yellow one to show similarities with the word *cat*.

Phonemic Awareness © 1997 Creative Teaching Press

All Aboard the Sound Train

Tasks: phoneme segmentation, phoneme isolation

Materials

- Boxcar Trains (page 116)
- picture cards (pages 77–100)
- overhead projector, transparency, and marker
- counters

Directions

1. Use a transparency to guide children through this activity. Give each child a Boxcar Train and five counters. Ask students to place a counter below each boxcar.

2. Have children pronounce picture names aloud, one at a time, either to you or a partner. Ask them to slide a counter into a boxcar with each sound they hear. (For example, for the boat picture, they would slide counters into three boxcars, one for each phoneme in the word.) Have more advanced learners write corresponding letters instead of using counters.

Phonemic Awareness © 1997 Creative Teaching Press

Zippity-Bippity

Task: phoneme substitution

Materials

- none

Directions

1. Teach children the following verse to the tune of "Zippity-Do-Dah."

> *Bippity-bo-bah, Bippity-bay,*
> *My, oh my, what a wonderful day.*
> *Plenty of sunshine coming my way.*
> *Bippity-bo-bah, Bippity-bay.*

2. Have children repeat the song several times, substituting the initial sounds in the verse with other sounds. For example: *mippity-mo-mah, wippity-wo-wah, tippity-to-tah.*

Phonemic Awareness © 1997 Creative Teaching Press

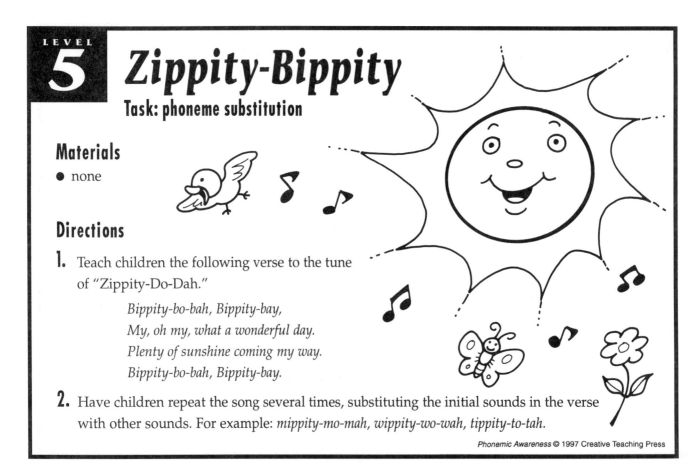

Animal Fun

Tasks: phoneme substitution, sound matching

Materials

● none

Directions

1. Teach the following verse to the tune of "Mary Had a Little Lamb."

> *Freddy **Frog** had a **log**,*
> *had a **log**,*
> *had a **log**,*
> *Freddy **Frog** had a **log**,*
> *He stayed and played all day.*

2. Repeat the verse using other alliterations (*Henry Hen, friend; Carlos Cat, hat; Polly Pig, twig; Sammy seal, wheel; Frieda Fox, box; Skitter Skunk, trunk*).

3. End with the verse, *Poor Charlie Chick, he was sick* (repeat). *He couldn't play all day!* Invite children to add their own alliterations to the song.

Phonemic Awareness © 1997 Creative Teaching Press

Circle Around the Sound

Task: phoneme substitution

Materials

● none

Directions

1. Divide the class into two groups, and have each group sit in a circle.

2. Choose a target ending sound such as /t/. Select a child from each group to start "passing the sound" by saying a word that ends with the target sound, such as *pet.* The next child to the left must then say another word with the same ending sound, such as *wet.*

3. If a child gives an incorrect response, have him or her sit behind someone else in the circle. Continue "moving the sound" to the left as individuals and partners say words that contain the target sound.

Phonemic Awareness © 1997 Creative Teaching Press

LEVEL 5

Change Your Partner

Tasks: phoneme deletion, phoneme substitution, phoneme blending

Materials

- words from current classroom literature
- Words within Words (page 117)

Directions

1. Invite three children to stand in a row. Secretly select a three-phoneme word and whisper beginning, middle, and ending sounds to the first, second, and third child.

2. Instruct each child to say his or her sound, and ask the class to blend the sounds to say a word. For example, Child 1 says, /p/, Child 2 says, /a/, Child 3 says, /t/—the class says, *pat*.

3. Assign other sounds to classmates and have them replace children in the row to form new words. For example replace /t/ with /n/ to change *pat* to *pan*. For variation, have children "beat the clock" as they decide which sounds to switch to create new words.

Phonemic Awareness © 1997 Creative Teaching Press

LEVEL 5

Drop Off, Add On

Tasks: phoneme deletion, phoneme substitution

Materials

- Words within Words (page 117)

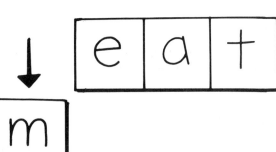

Directions

1. Read words from the word list one at a time. Ask children what sound needs to be dropped to uncover the "hidden word." For example, *What sound do you drop to change* meat *to* eat?

2. Increase the difficulty by using words with blends and clusters (*sweep* to *weep*, *craft* to *raft*, *glitter* to *litter*).

3. Vary the activity by having children add letters to given words (e.g., *Add /c/ to the beginning of* row *to make* _____).

Phonemic Awareness © 1997 Creative Teaching Press

Simon Says Sounds

abc ✏

Tasks: sound matching, matching letters to sounds

Materials

● alphabet cards (pages 118–120)

Directions

1. Divide the class into partners and give each pair a set of alphabet cards.

2. Play Simon Says using commands such as *Simon says touch the letter* F *with your pinky; Simon says place the letter that makes the /s/ sound on the floor; Place /d/ and /p/ letters on your shoe.*

3. Invite eliminated student pairs to sit near you and think of new commands for others.

Phonemic Awareness © 1997 Creative Teaching Press

We Are Family

abc ✏

Tasks: sound matching, matching sounds to letters

Materials

● We Are Family (pages 121–122)
● crayons or markers
● chart paper

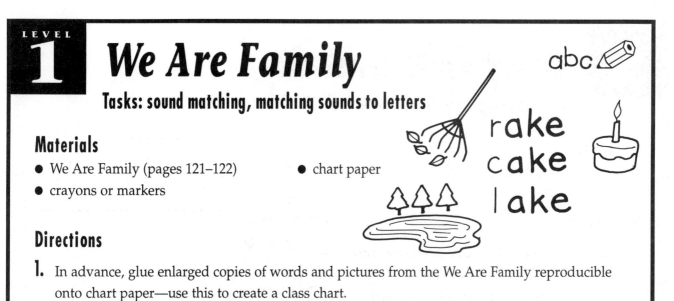

Directions

1. In advance, glue enlarged copies of words and pictures from the We Are Family reproducible onto chart paper—use this to create a class chart.

2. Distribute reproducibles and ask children to color common letters of rhyming words red and uncommon letters another color. For example, color letters *a, k, e* in words *cake* and *rake* red, letter *c* blue, and letter *r* green.

3. Have students complete their own reproducibles simultaneously as volunteers work on the class chart. Add new words to the class chart every few days.

Phonemic Awareness © 1997 Creative Teaching Press

Letter Hunt

abc

Tasks: sound matching, matching letters to sounds

Materials

- alphabet cards (pages 118–120)

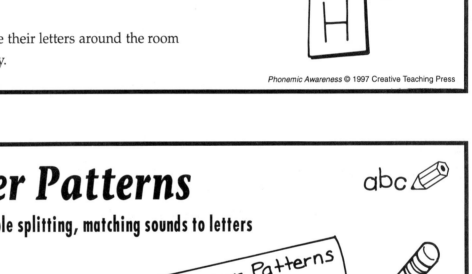

Directions

1. In advance, hide alphabet cards around the room.

2. Invite children to find a card, then sit down in a circle.

3. Have each child identify the sound that matches his or her letter, then say a word with that sound, such as *ball* for the letter *b*.

4. Invite children to hide their letters around the room and repeat the activity.

Phonemic Awareness © 1997 Creative Teaching Press

Letter Patterns

abc

Tasks: syllable splitting, matching sounds to letters

Materials

- Letter Patterns (page 123)
- crayons

Directions

1. Give a Letter Patterns reproducible to each child.

2. This is a visual scanning activity. Say a rime found in some of the words on the page (e.g., /at/). Have children use red crayons to circle the letters in each word that correspond to the sound.

3. Change the target rime to /ax/, /it/, /id/, /et/, /en/, /op/, /ot/, /ub/, or /ug/, and repeat the process. Ask children to use different-colored crayons for each pattern. After selecting three or four patterns, review the circled words by asking children to read all same-colored words.

Phonemic Awareness © 1997 Creative Teaching Press

Monster Puppets

abc

Tasks: phoneme blending, matching sounds to letters

Materials

- small paper bags
- glue
- crayons or markers
- craft supplies (construction paper, yarn, wiggly eyes)
- alphabet cards (pages 118–120)

Directions

1. Distribute supplies and have children decorate paper bags to make monster puppets. Glue a letter on the front of each puppet—be sure to use all letters of the alphabet.

2. Invite two volunteers to the front of the class to spell a two-letter word with their letter puppets (e.g., *me*). Tap each child on the shoulder and ask the class to give the sound of that puppet, then have children blend sounds together to say the word.

3. Repeat with new volunteers. As children achieve mastery, move on to three- and four-letter words.

Phonemic Awareness © 1997 Creative Teaching Press

Walkie-Talkie Friends

abc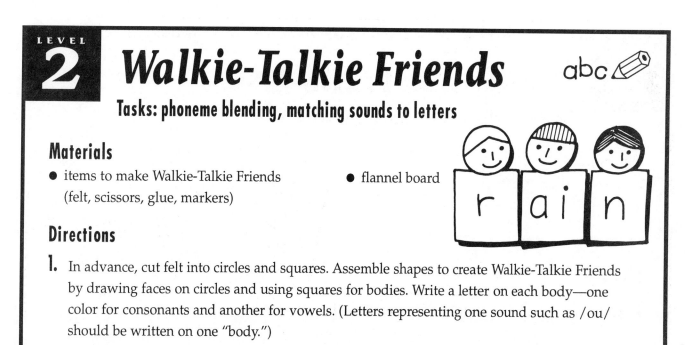

Tasks: phoneme blending, matching sounds to letters

Materials

- items to make Walkie-Talkie Friends (felt, scissors, glue, markers)
- flannel board

Directions

1. In advance, cut felt into circles and squares. Assemble shapes to create Walkie-Talkie Friends by drawing faces on circles and using squares for bodies. Write a letter on each body—one color for consonants and another for vowels. (Letters representing one sound such as /ou/ should be written on one "body.")

2. Create words by placing Walkie-Talkie Friends side by side on a flannel board, identifying individual sounds as you add each letter. Emphasize that when Walkie-Talkie Friends walk together, they talk together. Invite volunteers to "walk" their fingers under each Walkie-Talkie Friend as they blend the sounds to say the word.

Phonemic Awareness © 1997 Creative Teaching Press

Slip and Slide

abc

Tasks: phoneme blending, matching sounds to letters

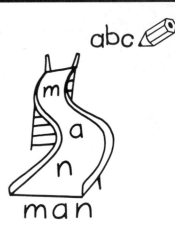

Materials

- Slip and Slide (page 124)
- magnetic board or cookie sheet
- magnetic letters
- pencils or crayons

Directions

1. Enlarge and attach a paper slide to a magnetic board. Place magnetic letters *m*, *a*, and *n* at the top, middle, and bottom of the slide, corresponding to letter-positioning in the word. Slide the *m* down to join the *a*, saying the sounds of the letters as you join them together. Then, slide both letters down to join the *n*, moving all three letters into the "pool" to spell and say the word *man*. Emphasize the continuous blending of sounds as you complete the process.

2. Distribute Slip and Slide reproducibles, and have children write letter positions on their slides as you repeat the process with new words. Have children move a finger down each slide as they blend the letter sounds aloud.

Phonemic Awareness © 1997 Creative Teaching Press

Choo-Choo Charlie

abc

Tasks: phoneme blending, matching sounds to letters

Materials

- words from current classroom literature
- toy or paper trains
- index cards
- marker

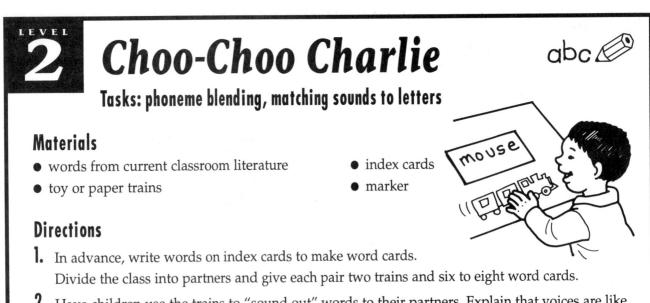

Directions

1. In advance, write words on index cards to make word cards. Divide the class into partners and give each pair two trains and six to eight word cards.

2. Have children use the trains to "sound out" words to their partners. Explain that voices are like the continuous movement of a train—they must extend and blend letter sounds as they slowly say the word. Have children slowly move a train from left to right below each letter on a card, saying the corresponding sounds.

3. When children finish reading their words, invite them to switch cards with another pair for additional practice.

Phonemic Awareness © 1997 Creative Teaching Press

Picture Puzzles

Tasks: phoneme blending, matching sounds to letters

Materials

- envelopes
- crayons or markers
- index cards
- scissors

Directions

1. Draw pictures or glue picture cutouts on envelopes, and write matching words on index cards.

2. Ask children to cut apart each word, letter by letter, in a zig-zag pattern to make puzzle pieces. Have them place words together while blending the phonemes aloud. Have children store puzzle pieces in matching envelopes.

3. Invite children to trade envelopes and repeat the process. Have more advanced learners make new puzzles using their own pictures and words.

Phonemic Awareness © 1997 Creative Teaching Press

Be the Sound

Tasks: phoneme blending, matching sounds to letters

Materials

- index cards
- marker

Directions

1. In advance, make letter cards for several simple words (e.g., letters *c*, *a*, and *t* for *cat*). Make enough cards so each child has at least one.

2. Call out the initial sound of a word (/c/ in *cat*) and have the child (or children) holding that letter come to the front. Continue calling other sounds in the word sequentially, lining children up from left to right.

3. When the word has been "built," ask each card holder to say his or her sound. Ask the rest of the class to blend the individual sounds to say the word. Repeat with new words until all children have had a turn.

Phonemic Awareness © 1997 Creative Teaching Press

Word Line

abc

Tasks: phoneme blending, matching sounds to letters

Materials

- words from current classroom literature
- chalkboard and chalk (white, colored)

Directions

1. Use colored chalk to write one vowel (*a*) on the board three times.
   (You will be building a separate word around each vowel.) Have children identify the letter.

2. Using white chalk, add the same initial consonant to each vowel (*ma*)—three identical versions.
   Have children say the letter sounds together.

3. Use different-colored chalk to add different ending consonants to each word in the line (e.g.,
   man, map, mad). Have children read the words.

4. Create more "word lines" on the board (*rat, ran, rag; fat, fast, faster*). Maintain a fast pace to hold
   children's attention.

Phonemic Awareness © 1997 Creative Teaching Press

Sort by Sound

abc

Tasks: phoneme isolation, matching sounds to letters

Materials

- bags of small objects (top, toothbrush, marble, mirror, dime)
- plastic letters or letter cards (three per student pair)

Directions

1. Distribute letters and objects to partners. Have them group objects
   by initial sounds, placing them under the corresponding letters. Have
   children place the objects that don't match the letters back in the bag.

2. Ask children to sort the objects again by middle or ending sounds,
   using the same letters. Have children share results with classmates.

3. Invite children to exchange letters or bags of objects and repeat
   the activity.

Phonemic Awareness © 1997 Creative Teaching Press

LEVEL 3 Color-Coded Reading

abc ✏️

Tasks: phoneme isolation, matching sounds to letters

Materials

- words from current classroom literature or General Words List (pages 70–73)
- index cards
- markers

Directions

1. Make color-coded word cards—one color for letter combinations that make the same sound (e.g., *ow* and *ou*) and another color for all other letters. For example, red for *ow* and *ou* in the words *cow* and *out*, and all other letters black.

2. Using only one "family," show a word card *(cow)*, and have children respond by saying only the color-coded sound of the word *(/ow/)*. Once children understand the process, show other cards in rapid succession.

3. After combinations are identified consistently, show the cards again. Have children read the word after the color-coded sound is identified. For example, *ow, cow*. Repeat with other words.

Phonemic Awareness © 1997 Creative Teaching Press

LEVEL 3 Photo Line

abc ✏️

Tasks: phoneme isolation, matching letters to sounds

Materials

- items to make photo cards (student photos, index cards, glue or tape, permanent marker)
- alphabet cards (pages 118–120)
- clothesline and pins

Directions

1. In advance, make photo cards by gluing or taping student pictures to index cards and writing the name of each student below his or her picture. Hang alphabet cards on a clothesline, leaving space between each letter.

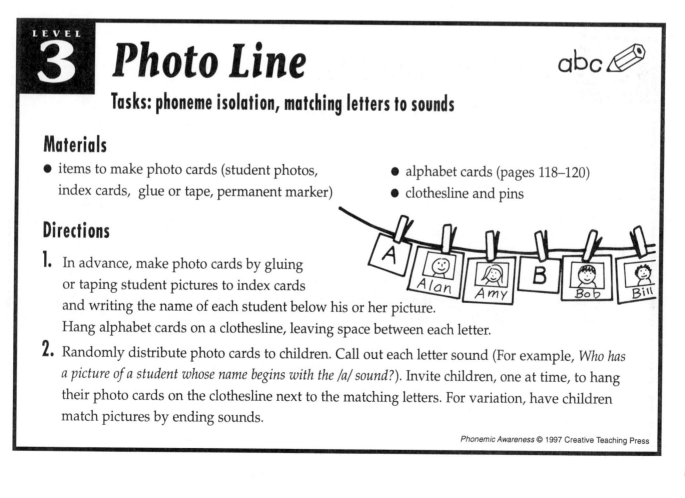

2. Randomly distribute photo cards to children. Call out each letter sound (For example, *Who has a picture of a student whose name begins with the /a/ sound?*). Invite children, one at time, to hang their photo cards on the clothesline next to the matching letters. For variation, have children match pictures by ending sounds.

Phonemic Awareness © 1997 Creative Teaching Press

Sound Relay

Tasks: phoneme isolation, matching sounds to letters

Materials
- bag of plastic letters (consonants)
- small objects (two for each consonant sound in the bag)

Directions

1. Place objects at the end of a playing field. Have children say in chorus the name of each object.

2. Divide the class into two teams and line them up single file at the starting line. Have the first child in each team select a letter from the bag. Those two children then run to the object pile, find objects that match their letter sounds, and take them to the end of the line.

3. Each team member takes a turn, then sits down when he or she returns to the end of the line. Encourage team members to assist each other when needed. When the relay is finished, have children share their choices.

Phonemic Awareness © 1997 Creative Teaching Press

Word Chain

Tasks: phoneme isolation, matching sounds to letters

Materials
- chalkboard and chalk

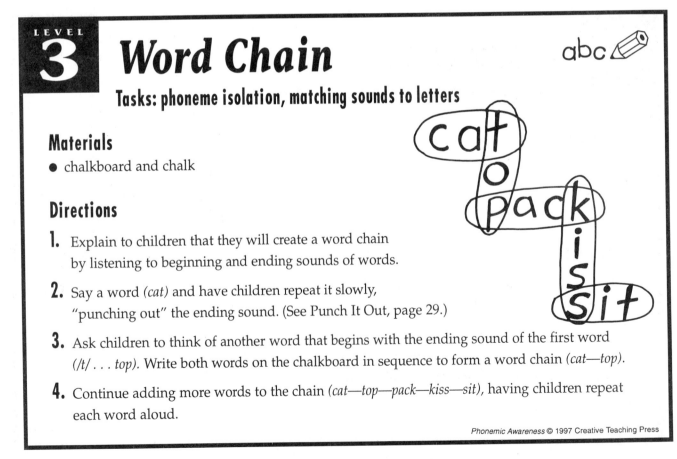

Directions

1. Explain to children that they will create a word chain by listening to beginning and ending sounds of words.

2. Say a word *(cat)* and have children repeat it slowly, "punching out" the ending sound. (See Punch It Out, page 29.)

3. Ask children to think of another word that begins with the ending sound of the first word *(/t/ . . . top)*. Write both words on the chalkboard in sequence to form a word chain *(cat—top)*.

4. Continue adding more words to the chain *(cat—top—pack—kiss—sit)*, having children repeat each word aloud.

Phonemic Awareness © 1997 Creative Teaching Press

LEVEL 4

Friendship Directory

abc ✏

Tasks: phoneme segmentation, phoneme blending, matching letters to sounds

Materials

- items to make Friendship Directories (unlined paper, stapler or paper rings, marker, student photos)

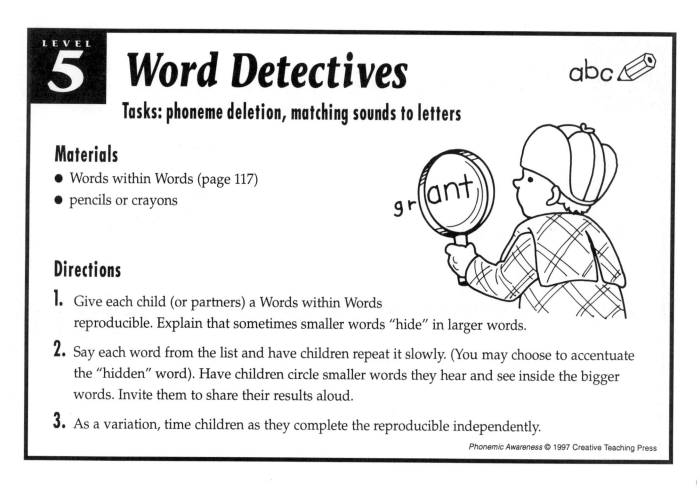

Directions

1. In advance, make one Friendship Directory for each child by writing each letter of the alphabet on separate pieces of paper and gluing student photos on the appropriate pages. (All students whose names begin with *A* have pictures pasted on the "A" page.) Copy directory pages and staple them together.

2. Each day, have children say, then write, three or four student names in their directories. First, have children point to a student's picture and say his or her name slowly. Next, ask children to identify the phonemes as you write corresponding letters on the chalkboard. Last, have them blend the letter sounds together as they write the student's name under his or her photograph.

Phonemic Awareness © 1997 Creative Teaching Press

LEVEL 5

Word Detectives

abc ✏

Tasks: phoneme deletion, matching sounds to letters

Materials

- Words within Words (page 117)
- pencils or crayons

Directions

1. Give each child (or partners) a Words within Words reproducible. Explain that sometimes smaller words "hide" in larger words.

2. Say each word from the list and have children repeat it slowly. (You may choose to accentuate the "hidden" word). Have children circle smaller words they hear and see inside the bigger words. Invite them to share their results aloud.

3. As a variation, time children as they complete the reproducible independently.

Phonemic Awareness © 1997 Creative Teaching Press

Change That Vowel!

Tasks: phoneme substitution, phoneme blending, matching sounds to letters

Materials

- words from current classroom literature or General Words List (pages 70–73)
- alphabet cards (pages 118–120)
- pocket chart

Directions

1. Choose a one-syllable word (e.g., *big*) and place each letter, one by one, in a pocket chart. Have children say each phoneme separately as you place letters in the chart, then blend the sounds together to form the word.

2. Use other vowel cards to replace the middle sound, creating new words (*beg, bag, bog, bug*). Discuss whether words created make sense or are "nonsense" words.

3. Repeat with other one-syllable words.

Phonemic Awareness © 1997 Creative Teaching Press

Sound Switch

abc

Tasks: phoneme substitution, phoneme blending, matching sounds to letters

Materials

- large alphabet cards (two sets)
- pocket chart

Directions

1. Place letters in a pocket chart to form a simple one-syllable word (e.g., *cat*). Distribute other letters to students.

2. Point to each letter in the pocket chart and have the class say the sound. Ask children to blend the sounds together to form the word.

3. Invite volunteers to create new words by placing their letters over those in the pocket chart, such as placing the letter *m* over *c* to form the word *mat*. Have children blend the new sounds together and decide whether or not the new word makes sense.

4. Place new one-syllable words in the pocket chart and repeat the process.

Phonemic Awareness © 1997 Creative Teaching Press

LEVEL 5

Rhyming Zig-Zag

abc ✏️

Tasks: phoneme substitution, phoneme blending, matching sounds to letters

Materials
● rhyming picture cards (pages 77–88)

Directions

1. Place students in two lines facing each other. Give each person a picture card.

2. Choose one student at the end of a line to start the activity. Have him or her show his or her picture card (e.g., boat), then give a "replacement" letter for the beginning sound (e.g., c).

3. Ask the student standing directly across in the opposite line to say the new word made by changing the first letter *(coat)*. He or she then continues the process by showing his or her picture card to the next person and giving a replacement letter.

4. Have students continue the zig-zag process until everyone has a turn. As an extra challenge, time students and invite them to "beat the clock."

Phonemic Awareness © 1997 Creative Teaching Press

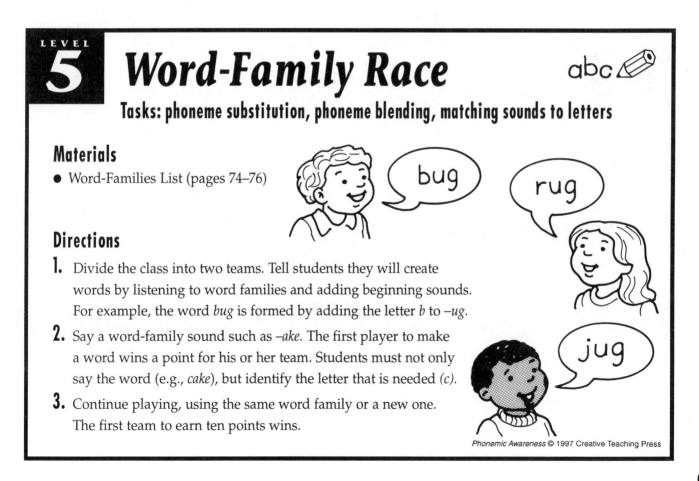

LEVEL 5

Word-Family Race

abc ✏️

Tasks: phoneme substitution, phoneme blending, matching sounds to letters

Materials
● Word-Families List (pages 74–76)

Directions

1. Divide the class into two teams. Tell students they will create words by listening to word families and adding beginning sounds. For example, the word *bug* is formed by adding the letter *b* to –*ug*.

2. Say a word-family sound such as –*ake*. The first player to make a word wins a point for his or her team. Students must not only say the word (e.g., *cake*), but identify the letter that is needed *(c)*.

3. Continue playing, using the same word family or a new one. The first team to earn ten points wins.

Phonemic Awareness © 1997 Creative Teaching Press

Alphabet House

abc

Tasks: phoneme substitution, phoneme deletion, phoneme isolation, phoneme blending, matching sounds to letters

Materials

- items to make alphabet house (construction paper, scissors, tape, metal cookie sheet)
- magnetic letters

Directions

1. In advance, cut out a construction-paper house. Cut three adjacent windows below the roof. Tape the house to a cookie sheet.

2. Display magnetic letters on the rooftop. Bring down three letters, placing one in each window to spell a word. Have children isolate and blend the phonemes together to say the word. Show children how to substitute and delete phonemes to create new words (e.g., *bat* to *cat* or *at*).

Phonemic Awareness © 1997 Creative Teaching Press

LEVEL 5

Build a Word

abc

Tasks: phoneme substitution, phoneme deletion, phoneme isolation, phoneme blending, matching sounds to letters

Materials

- letter cards t, a, n, i, g, s (one set per child)
- Build a Word—Teacher's Script (page 125)

Add one letter to make "at" say "ant."

Directions

1. Distribute letter cards. Review the name and sound for each letter.

2. Invite children to freely explore letters, encouraging them to create simple words (e.g., *it, an, in*).

3. Ask children to listen to your directions and make words. Read the Build a Word—Teacher's Script aloud, stopping after each sentence to give students time to build the words. Circulate around the room as you read, making sure children are following along. Offer prompts when needed, and invite children to share answers after each step.

Phonemic Awareness © 1997 Creative Teaching Press

Phonemic-Awareness Inventory

Student Name _____   Date _____

Directions: Give this inventory orally to each student.

1 Level 1

Whole Word Discrimination

Are these words the same? (Circle words child identifies correctly.)

fat–bat	red–rid	slip–slit
dip–hip	nut–nut	grip–grip
man–man	mat–map	flit–flip

Rhyming Words—Recognition

Do these words rhyme? (Circle words child identifies correctly.)

happy–sappy	boy–toy	sun–fun
sad–mad	girl–boy	play–game

Rhyming Words—Application

What word rhymes with . . . ? (Write child's responses on the lines.)

man _____   old _____   try_____

sun _____   play _____   skip _____

eat _____   book _____   scale _____

Syllable Counting

How many syllables do you hear in the word . . . ? (Write child's responses on the lines and circle those that are correct.)

ball _____   wagon _____   umbrella _____

elephant _____   hippopotamus _____   orangutan _____

 Level 2

Syllable Segmentation

I'll say a word, then you repeat it slowly. (Give examples: *cow–boy, ha–ppy, fu–nny*. Circle words to which child responds correctly.)

rainbow (rain–bow)	paper (pa–per)	scissors (sci–ssors)
doughnut (dough–nut)	basket (bas–ket)	butterfly (bu–tter–fly)
sidewalk (side–walk)	color (co–lor)	umbrella (um–bre–lla)

Oral Synthesis—Blending Speech Sounds

Listen and tell me the word I said. (Say each sound slowly. Circle words child identifies correctly.)

n–o	r–u–n	t–e–n	w–a–s	c–a–k–e
s–ay	f–a–t	c–u–t	h–a–ve	w–e–n–t
m–e	s–i–t	m–o–p	s–ai–d	st–o–r–y

Level 3

Approximation

Do you hear the /b/ sound at the beginning, middle, or end of _____? (Circle words child identifies correctly.)

big	robot	banana
tab	cabbage	crib

Phoneme Isolation

What sound do you hear _____? (Circle words child identifies correctly.)

First	Last	Middle
sun	water	feet
foot	buff	tub
yes	candy	lake
red	ten	pan

68

Phonemic Awareness © 1997 Creative Teaching Press

4 Level 4

Segmentation

Repeat each word slowly so I can hear each separate sound, like c–a–t. (Say a word and have child repeat it slowly, separating each phoneme.)

me	you	book
so	play	skip
man	old	scale

5 Level 5

Phoneme Deletion

Say the word _____, but leave off the _____. (Repeat, asking child to delete beginning or ending sounds.)

pop	dip	not	cub	fin
can	ten	tab	mop	set

Phoneme Substitution

Replace the first sound in _____ with _____. What is the new word? (Repeat, asking child to substitute middle and ending sounds.)

pail	log	get
cat	tub	pop
pig	dice	jump

General Words List

Use this word list to supplement those generated from current classroom literature.

Words	Onsets	Rimes	Phonemes
a	none	–a	/a/
all	none	–all	/a/ /l/
am	none	–am	/a/ /m/
an	none	–an	/a/ /n/
and	none	–and	/a/ /n/ /d/
are	none	–are	/ar/
as	none	–as	/a/ /s/
ask	none	–ask	/a/ /s/ /k/
at	none	–at	/a/ /t/
ate	none	–ate	/ā/ /t/
ball	b–	–all	/b/ /a/ /l/
barn	b–	–arn	/b/ /ar/ /n/
be	b–	–e	/b/ /ē/
bed	b–	–ed	/b/ /e/ /d/
bell	b–	–ell	/b/ /e/ /l/
big	b–	–ig	/b/ /i/ /g/
bird	b–	–ird	/b/ /ir/ /d/
black	bl–	–ack	/b/ /l/ /a/ /k/
blue	bl–	–ue	/b/ /l/ /ū/
boat	b–	–oat	/b/ /ō/ /t/
boy	b–	–oy	/b/ /oy/
brown	br–	–own	/b/ /r/ /ow/ /n/
but	b–	–ut	/b/ /u/ /t/
by	b–	–y	/b/ /ī/
call	c–	–all	/c/ /a/ /l/
came	c–	–ame	/c/ /ā/ /m/
can	c–	–an	/c/ /a/ /n/
cap	c–	–ap	/c/ /a/ /p/
car	c–	–ar	/c/ /ar/
cat	c–	–at	/c/ /a/ /t/

Phonemic Awareness © 1997 Creative Teaching Press

General Words List

Words	Onsets	Rimes	Phonemes
cow	c–	–ow	/c/ /ow/
day	d–	–ay	/d/ /ā/
did	d–	–id	/d/ /i/ /d/
do	d–	–o	/d/ /o/
dog	d–	–og	/d/ /o/ /g/
doll	d–	–oll	/d/ /o/ /l/
down	d–	–own	/d/ /ow/ /n/
duck	d–	–uck	/d/ /u/ /k/
eat	none	–eat	/ē/ /t/
farm	f–	–arm	/f/ /ar/ /m/
feet	f–	–eet	/f/ /ē/ /t/
find	f–	–ind	/f/ /i/ /n/ /d/
for	f–	–or	/f/ /or/
frog	fr–	–og	/f/ /r/ /o/ /g/
girl	g–	–irl	/g/ /ir/ /l/
give	g–	–ive	/g/ /i/ /v/
go	g–	–o	/g/ /o/
good	g–	–ood	/g/ /oo/ /d/
green	gr–	–een	/g/ /r/ /ē/ /n/
had	h–	–ad	/h/ /a/ /d/
has	h–	–as	/h/ /a/ /s/
hat	h–	–at	/h/ /a/ /t/
have	h–	–ave	/h/ /a/ /v/
he	h–	–e	/h/ /ē/
help	h–	–elp	/h/ /e/ /l/ /p/
hen	h–	–en	/h/ /e/ /n/
her	h–	–er	/h/ /er/
here	h–	–ere	/h/ /ē/ /r/
him	h–	–im	/h/ /i/ /m/
horse	h–	–orse	/h/ /or/ /s/
house	h–	–ouse	/h/ /ou/ /s/

General Words List

Words	Onsets	Rimes	Phonemes
how	h–	–ow	/h/ /o/ /w/
I	none	–i	/ī/
if	none	–if	/i/ /f/
in	none	–in	/i/ /n/
is	none	–is	/i/ /s/
it	none	–it	/i/ /t/
jump	j–	–ump	/j/ /u/ /m/ /p/
king	k–	–ing	/k/ /i/ /ng/
let	l–	–et	/l/ /e/ /t/
like	l–	–ike	/l/ /ī/ /k/
look	l–	–ook	/l/ /oo/ /k/
mad	m–	–ad	/m/ /a/ /d/
make	m–	–ake	/m/ /ā/ /k/
man	m–	–an	/m/ /a/ /n/
me	m–	–e	/m/ /ē/
mouse	m–	–ouse	/m/ /ou/ /s/
must	m–	–ust	/m/ /u/ /s/ /t/
my	m–	–y	/m/ /ī/
new	n–	–ew	/n/ /ew/
no	n–	–o	/n/ /ō/
not	n–	–ot	/n/ /o/ /t/
now	n–	–ow	/n/ /ow/
of	none	–of	/o/ /f/
old	none	–old	/ō/ /l/ /d/
on	none	–on	/o/ /n/
or	none	–or	/or/
out	none	–out	/ou/ /t/
pick	p–	–ick	/p/ /i/ /k/
pig	p–	–ig	/p/ /i/ /g/
play	pl–	–ay	/p/ /l/ /ā/
put	p–	–ut	/p/ /u/ /t/
ran	r–	–an	/r/ /a/ /n/

Phonemic Awareness © 1997 Creative Teaching Press

General Words List

Words	Onsets	Rimes	Phonemes
red	r–	–ed	/r/ /e/ /d/
ride	r–	–ide	/r/ /ī/ /d/
run	r–	–un	/r/ /u/ /n/
sad	s–	–ad	/s/ /a/ /d/
said	s–	–aid	/s/ /ai/ /d/
saw	s–	–aw	/s/ /aw/
say	s–	–ay	/s/ /ā/
see	s–	–ee	/s/ /ē/
she	sh–	–e	/sh/ /ē/
sing	s–	–ing	/s/ /i/ /ng/
sit	s–	–it	/s/ /i/ /t/
sleep	sl–	–eep	/s/ /l/ /ē/ /p/
so	s–	–o	/s/ /ō/
stop	st–	–op	/s/ /t/ /o/ /p/
tell	t–	–ell	/t/ /e/ /l/
that	th–	–at	/th/ /a/ /t/
the	th–	–e	/th/ /e/
them	th–	–em	/th/ /e/ /m/
then	th–	–en	/th/ /e/ /n/
they	th–	–ey	/th/ /ey/
this	th–	–is	/th/ /i/ /s/
three	thr–	–ee	/th/ /r/ /ē/
to	t–	–o	/t/ /o/
top	t–	–op	/t/ /o/ /p/
up	none	–up	/u/ /p/
us	none	–us	/u/ /s/
we	w–	–e	/w/ /ē/
well	w–	–ell	/w/ /e/ /l/
will	w–	–ill	/w/ /i/ /l/
with	w–	–ith	/w/ /i/ /th/
work	w–	–ork	/w/ /or/ /k/
yes	y–	–es	/y/ /e/ /s/

Word-Families List–Short Vowels

–ack: back, jack, pack, rack, sack, tack, black, clack, crack, quack, shack, snack, track

–ad: bad, dad, had, lad, mad, pad, sad, glad

–ag: bag, gag, lag, nag, rag, sag, tag, wag, drag, flag, shag, snag

–am: dam, ham, jam, ram, cram, slam, wham

–an: ban, can, fan, man, pan, ran, tan, van, plan, scan

–ap: cap, gap, lap, map, nap, rap, sap, tap, clap, flap, slap, snap, trap

–at: at, bat, cat, fat, hat, mat, pat, rat, sat, vat, flat, that

–ed: bed, fed, led, red, wed, bred, fled, shed, sled, sped, shred

–ell: bell, cell, fell, sell, well, shell, smell, spell

–en: den, hen, men, pen, ten, then, when, wren

–est: best, jest, nest, rest, vest, west, chest, quest

–et: bet, get, jet, let, met, net, pet, set, vet, wet, yet, fret

–ick: kick, lick, pick, sick, tick, wick, brick, chick, quick, slick, stick, thick, trick

–id: did, hid, kid, lid, rid, slid, squid

–ig: big, dig, fig, jig, pig, rig, wig, twig

–ill: bill, dill, fill, gill, hill, mill, pill, sill, will, chill, drill, frill, grill, skill, spill, still, thrill

Phonemic Awareness © 1997 Creative Teaching Press

Word-Families List—Short Vowels

–in: fin, kin, pin, tin, win, chin, grin, skin, spin, thin, twin

–ing: king, ring, sing, wing, bring, cling, sling, sting, swing, thing, spring, string,

–ink: link, mink, pink, rink, sink, wink, blink, drink, stink, think, shrink

–ip: dip, hip, nip, sip, tip, chip, drip, flip, grip, ship, skip, slip, trip, whip

–it: bit, fit, hit, kit, lit, pit, sit, wit, grit, knit, quit, skit, slit, split

–ock: dock, lock, rock, sock, clock, flock, knock, shock, smock, stock

–og: dog, fog, hog, jog, log, clog, frog, smog

–op: hop, mop, pop, top, chop, drop, shop, stop

–ot: cot, dot, hot, lot, not, pot, rot, tot, knot, plot, spot, trot

–ub: dub, cub, hub, rub, sub, tub, club, grub, stub, scrub, shrub

–uck: buck, duck, luck, puck, suck, tuck, chuck, cluck, stuck, truck, struck

–ug: bug, dug, hug, jug, mug, rug, tug, drug, plug, slug, snug

–um: bum, gum, hum, sum, drum, plum

–un: bun, fun, nun, pun, run, sun, spun

–ut: cut, jut, nut, rut, shut, strut

Word-Families List—Long Vowels

–ail: bail, fail, hail, jail, mail, nail, pail, rail, sail, tail, wail, frail, quail, snail, trail

–ain: gain, main, pain, rain, brain, chain, drain, grain, stain, train

–ake: bake, cake, lake, make, rake, take, wake, brake, flake, shake, snake, stake

–ame: came, fame, game, lame, same, tame, blame, flame

–ank: bank, rank, sank, tank, blank, clank, crank, flank, plank, spank, thank

–ate: fate, gate, late, mate, plate, skate, state

–eat: beat, heat, meat, neat, seat, treat, wheat

–eep: beep, deep, jeep, keep, peep, weep, creep, sheep, sleep, steep, sweep

–eet: feet, meet, sheet, sleet, sweet, street

–ice: dice, lice, mice, nice, rice, price, slice, spice, twice

–ide: hide, ride, side, tide, wide, bride, glide, pride, slide

–ime: dime, lime, mime, time, crime, prime

–ive: dive, five, hive, live, drive

–oat: boat, coat, goat, bloat, float, gloat, throat

–old: bold, cold, gold, hold, mold, sold, told

–ole: hole, mole, pole, stole, whole

–one: bone, cone, tone, zone, phone, stone

–ose: hose, nose, rose, close, those

–y: by, my, cry, fly, fry, ply, sly, try, why

Phonemic Awareness © 1997 Creative Teaching Press

Rhyming Picture Cards

chick, stick; duck, truck; bug, rug

Rhyming Picture Cards

skunk, trunk; fox, box; pig, big

Rhyming Picture Cards

dog, frog; mouse, house; ski, tree

Rhyming Picture Cards

tail, whale; cat, rat; snake, cake

Phonemic Awareness © 1997 Creative Teaching Press

Rhyming Picture Cards

train, chain; run, sun; fan, pan

Rhyming Picture Cards

hide, slide; mop, hop; hook, cook

Rhyming Picture Cards

jar, car; top, drop; bag, flag

Rhyming Picture Cards

goat, coat; horn, corn; rope, soap

Rhyming Picture Cards

clap, map, snap; kite, bite, light

Rhyming Picture Cards

paw, saw, draw; feet, wheat, street

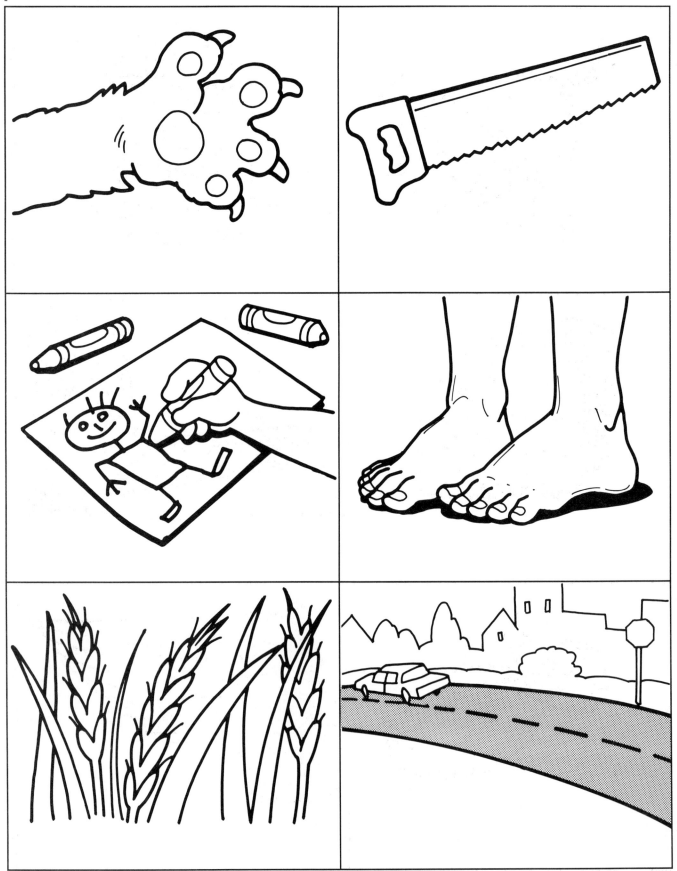

Rhyming Picture Cards

bell, well, shell; swing, ring, wing

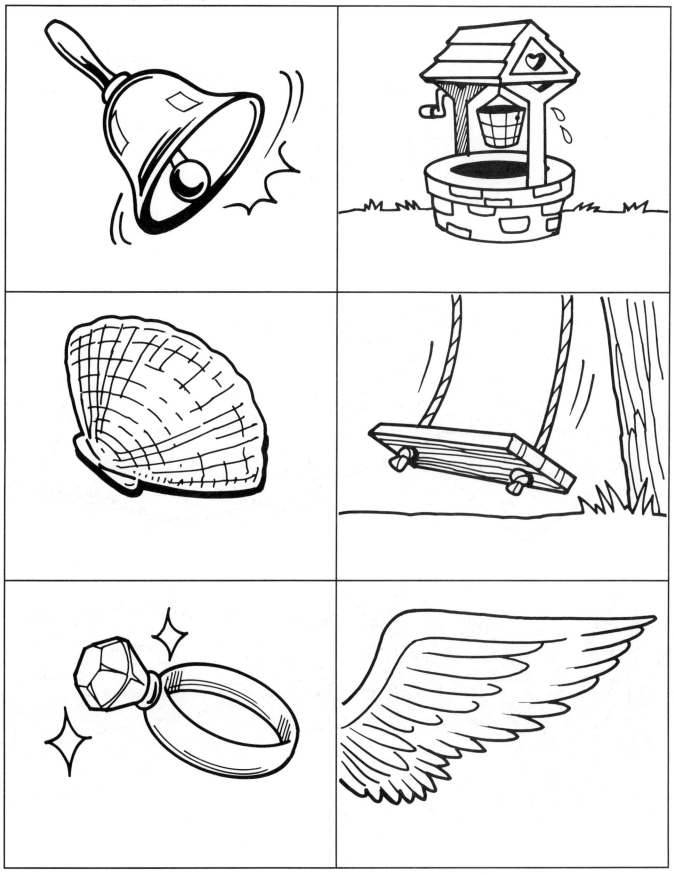

Rhyming Picture Cards

lock, block, rock, clock, knock, sock

Phonemic Awareness © 1997 Creative Teaching Press

Multiple-Syllable Picture Cards

butterfly, dinosaur, octopus, alligator, elephant, caterpillar

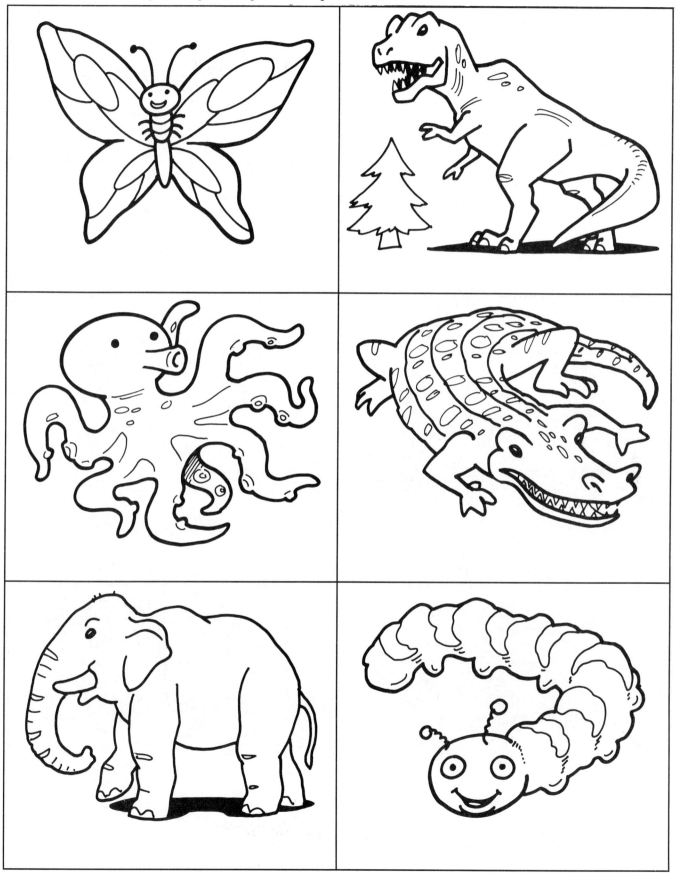

Multiple-Syllable Picture Cards

hippopotamus, rhinoceros, harmonica, submarine, helicopter, umbrella

Two-Phoneme Picture Cards

pie, toe, knee, tea, ice, key

Two-Phoneme Picture Cards

sew, bee, bow, hay, pea, egg

Three-Phoneme Picture Cards

bat, cup, phone, boat, book, ball

Three-Phoneme Picture Cards

bike, pin, leaf, fish, nail, hose

Phonemic Awareness © 1997 Creative Teaching Press

Four-Phoneme Picture Cards

star, drum, ladder, lamp, mask, turtle

Four-Phoneme Picture Cards

tiger, baby, penny, paper, hand, bottle

Four-Phoneme Picture Cards

spoon, plane, tent, fork, paint, snail

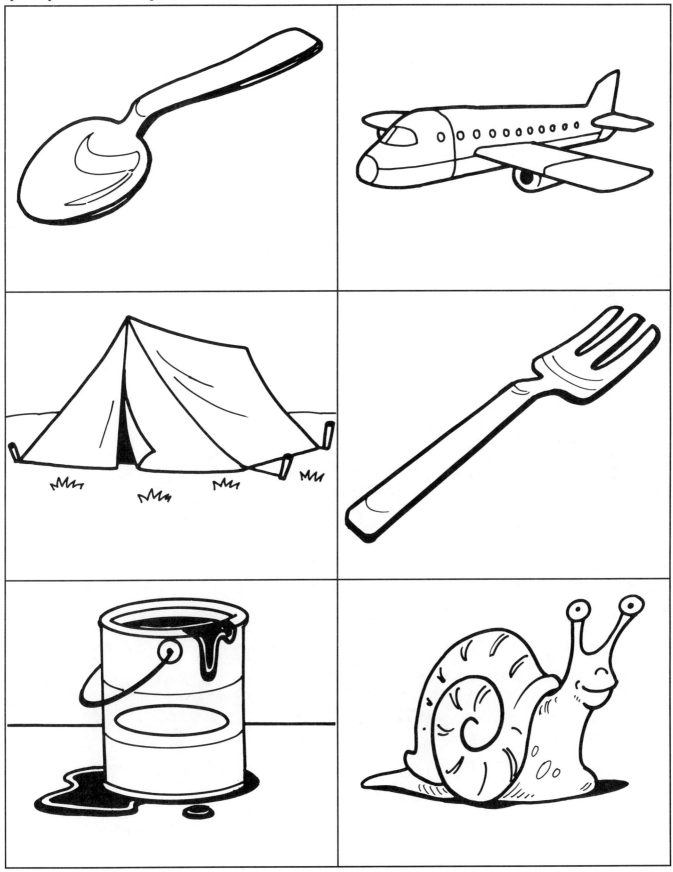

Five-Phoneme Picture Cards

gorilla, bucket, zebra, robot, lizard, peanut

Five-Phoneme Picture Cards

puppet, candy, rainbow, icicle, koala, raccoon

Five-Phoneme Picture Cards

rabbit, ticket, plant, rooster, cracker, lettuce

Phonemic Awareness © 1997 Creative Teaching Press

Rhyming Sentences

Look at that man
jump over the _____. (can, pan, fan)

See the frog
sit on a _____. (log, dog, hog, polliwog)

Did you ever see a whale
with a polka-dot _____? (tail, pail, snail, nail)

Look what I see!
A yellow and black _____. (bumblebee, tree)

Do you see the fly
sitting on the _____? (pie, tie)

Can you imagine a bear
with purple and green _____? (hair)

Watch the cat
playing with the _____. (rat, bat, hat, mat)

See the bug
holding a _____. (jug, mug, rug)

Can you imagine pigs
wearing _____? (wigs, figs, twigs)

Look up in the sky
and see a bird flying _____. (high, by)

See the little mouse
run through the _____. (house, blouse)

Look at the girl
with the big, brown _____. (curl, squirrel)

"O.K.," said dad,
"I'm really _____. (sad, mad, glad)

The clumsy ox
tripped over the _____. (box, fox, clocks, rocks, blocks)

Phonemic Awareness © 1997 Creative Teaching Press

Rhyme-Away Story 1

Directions: Draw the picture below on the chalkboard. Have students fill in the missing rhymes, then erase the corresponding portions of the picture.

Just for fun,
erase the <u>sun</u>.

If you can count to three,
erase the <u>tree</u>.

If you can count to four,
erase the <u>door</u>.

So you don't get stung by a bee,
erase the <u>chimney</u>.

If you can do so,
erase the <u>window</u>.

If you see a hound,
erase the <u>ground</u>.

A dog can say, "Woof,"
erase the <u>roof</u>.

Climb the tower,
erase the <u>flower</u>.

If you have five cents,
erase the <u>fence</u>.

If you see a doe,
erase another <u>window</u>.

You need power,
to erase another <u>flower</u>.

If you see a mouse,
erase the <u>house</u>.

Phonemic Awareness © 1997 Creative Teaching Press

Rhyme-Away Story 2

Directions: Draw the picture below on the chalkboard. Have students fill in the missing rhymes, then erase the corresponding portions of the picture.

He can't smell a rose,
if you erase his <u>nose</u>.

He can't play in a band,
if you erase his <u>hand</u>.

He doesn't wear a tie,
erase an <u>eye</u>.

He doesn't care,
if you erase his <u>hair</u>.

Don't ask why,
erase his other <u>eye</u>.

Never fear,
erase an <u>ear</u>.

He'll be a real wreck,
if you erase his <u>neck</u>.

He won't feel heat,
if you erase his <u>feet</u>.

It won't hurt,
if you erase his <u>shirt</u>.

He can't dance,
if you erase his <u>pants</u>.

He can go to bed,
if you erase his <u>head</u>.

Rhyme-Away Story 3

Directions: Draw the picture below on the chalkboard. Have students fill in the missing rhymes, then erase the corresponding portions of the picture.

I don't know how you feel,
but you can erase a <u>wheel</u>.

He ran to a fire,
erase a <u>tire</u>.

I have a friend named Thumper,
you can erase a <u>bumper</u>.

You can't see at night,
if you erase a <u>light</u>.

If you can count one, two, three, four,
you can erase a <u>door</u>.

A baby wears a diaper,
erase a <u>wiper</u>.

If you have ten toes,
you can erase the <u>windows</u>.

A dog says, "Woof, woof,"
erase the <u>roof</u>.

It looks a bit shoddy,
so erase the <u>body</u>.

Phonemic Awareness © 1997 Creative Teaching Press

Draw-a-Rhyme Story 1

Directions: Tell children they are going to draw a chalk picture together. Read each rhyme with the underlined words left out. Have children fill in the blanks (either orally or in writing), then add those parts to the chalkboard drawing.

When you draw a monster, it is said,
you always begin with his <u>head</u>.

He'll be able to see when he flies,
if we draw two bright <u>eyes</u>.

To tell which way the cold wind blows,
our monster will need a great big <u>nose</u>.

Look to the north and look to the south,
now we can give our monster a <u>mouth</u>.

Some up above and some beneath,
our monster has lots of <u>teeth</u>.

Now, under his chin, let's just check,
that's where we should put his <u>neck</u>.

So he won't be tipsy-toddy,
let's give him a polka-dot <u>body</u>.

If he really, really begs,
I guess we could give him <u>legs</u>.

To make our monster nice and neat,
we'll have to teach him to wipe his <u>feet</u>.

A notice sent by air mail!
We can't forget the monster's <u>tail</u>.

He isn't fierce, he isn't hairy,
but don't you think he's a little <u>scary</u>?

Draw-a-Rhyme Story 2

Directions: Tell children they are going to draw a chalk picture together. Read each rhyme with the underlined words left out. Have children fill in the blanks (either orally or in writing), then add those parts to the chalkboard drawing.

When making a clown, it is said,
always start with his big, round <u>head</u>.

Make it real messy 'cuz clowns don't care.
On the top of his head, give him red curly <u>hair</u>.

When people laugh, he wants to hear,
so on each side, give him a great big <u>ear</u>.

Now make him look very wise,
by giving him two wide-open <u>eyes</u>.

And yes, of course, everyone knows,
give him a big, fat, rounded <u>nose</u>.

Now make a line as long as a mile,
and turn it into a great big <u>smile</u>.

Look at his clothes—the clown suit he's in,
it has a ruffle right under his <u>chin</u>.

All over his suit are big colored spots,
so give him lots of <u>polka-dots</u>.

Now look at that, can you believe?
He has purple stripes on each long <u>sleeve</u>.

He has two hands—one left, one right,
one's painted yellow, and the other <u>white</u>.

At the bottom of his funny suit,
you can see one big, black <u>boot</u>.

And the other foot has not a shoe,
'cuz he just painted his toenails <u>blue</u>.

Now, if you listened and did everything right,
your little clown is a funny <u>sight</u>!

106

Phonemic Awareness © 1997 Creative Teaching Press

Draw-a-Rhyme Story 3

Directions: Tell children they are going to draw a chalk picture together. Read each rhyme with the underlined words left out. Have children fill in the blanks (either orally or in writing), then add those parts to the chalkboard drawing.

When drawing a Martian, it is said,
always start by making his <u>head</u>.

Don't give him hair on top of his head,
give him a shiny, round helmet that's <u>red</u>.

Look at his eyes, so scary and mean,
since he's from Mars, they must be <u>green</u>.

Right by his nose his eyeballs hide,
'cuz he just happens to be <u>cross-eyed</u>.

Just look at his nose, can you imagine that!
It has three holes and it's really <u>flat</u>.

His mouth is crooked with lots of teeth,
jagged on top and flat <u>underneath</u>.

Not only is his neck double-jointed,
but look at his ears—they're <u>pointed</u>!

I'm sure he has a body like you and me,
but a Martian's space suit is all you <u>see</u>.

Now, remember Martians are not to be feared,
they're not really dangerous, they just look kind of <u>weird</u>!

Turtle Talk

Bingo Record Sheet

/t/ _____

/l/ _____

/i/ _____

/f/ _____

/s/ _____

/o/ _____

/m/ _____

/g/ _____

/d/ _____

/p/ _____

/a/ _____

/r/ _____

/u/ _____

/e/ _____

/k/ _____

/n/ _____

/b/ _____

/v/ _____

/w/ _____

/h/ _____

Bingo Game Card

Sound Cards

/t/	/v/	/g/	/a/	/e/
/l/	/s/	/b/	/r/	/k/
/i/	/o/	/d/	/w/	/n/
/f/	/m/	/p/	/u/	/h/

Sound Dominos

Phonemic Awareness © 1997 Creative Teaching Press

Puppet Patterns

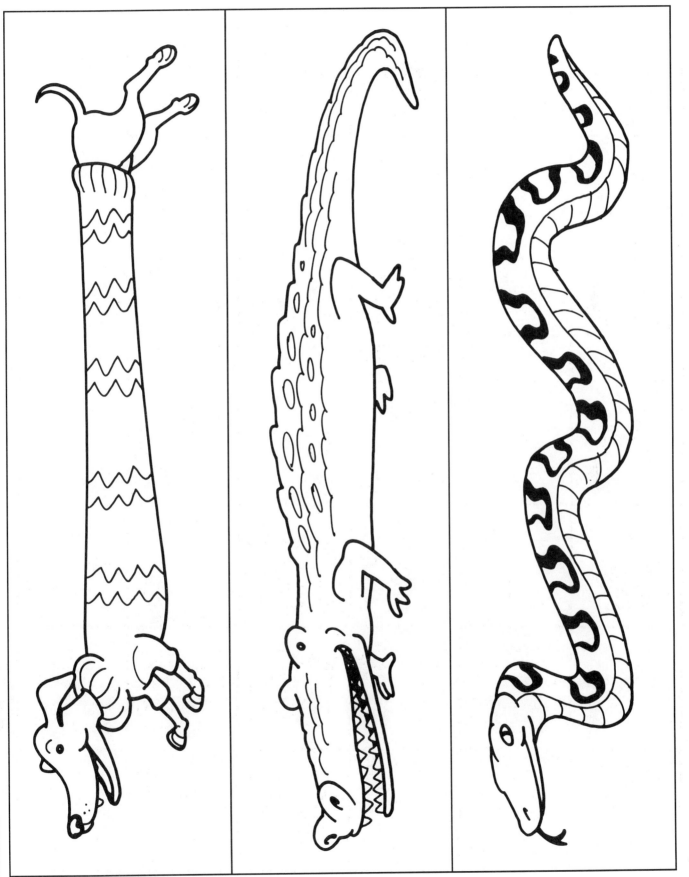

Froggy Hop

Phonemic Awareness © 1997 Creative Teaching Press

Sound Tree

Boxcar Trains

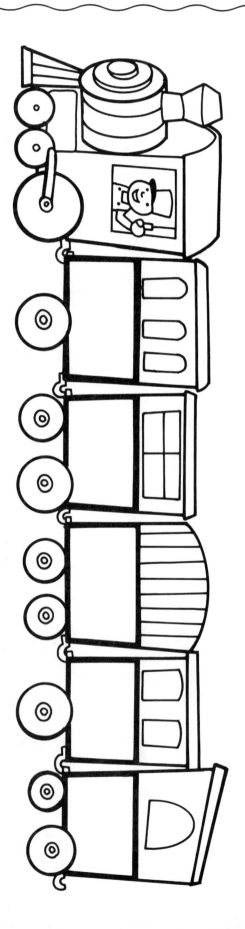
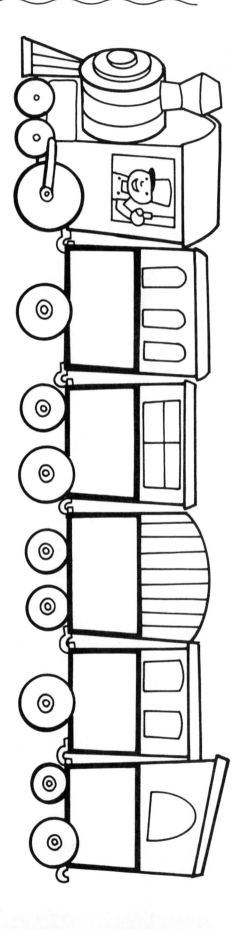

Phonemic Awareness © 1997 Creative Teaching Press

Words within Words

Student Name _____ Date _____

will	fast	ball	candy	fist
then	that	must	call	slip
meat	cold	wins	tent	plant
bus	done	fit	chill	pink
this	list	onto	boxer	stop
sled	pond	horn	inch	fond
twig	skin	grant	mend	pout
clap	hand	twin	farm	upset

Alphabet Cards

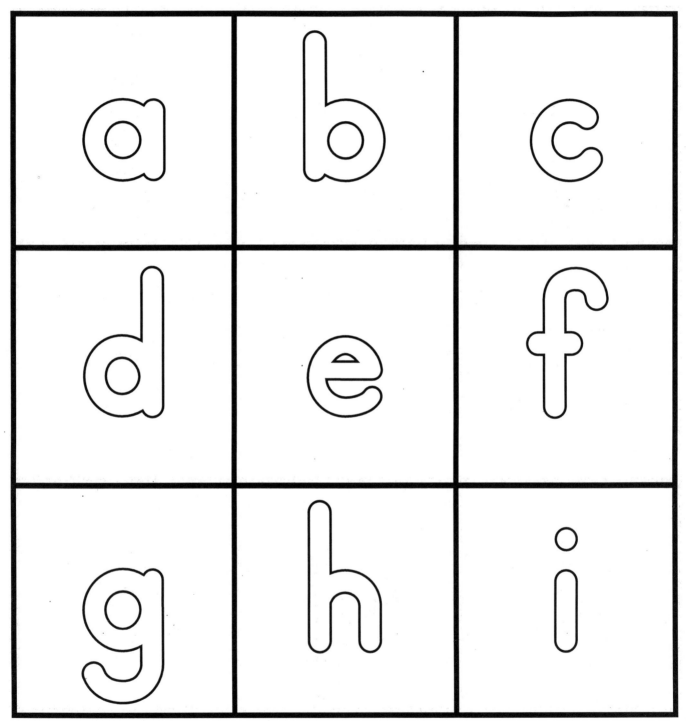

Phonemic Awareness © 1997 Creative Teaching Press

Alphabet Cards

Alphabet Cards

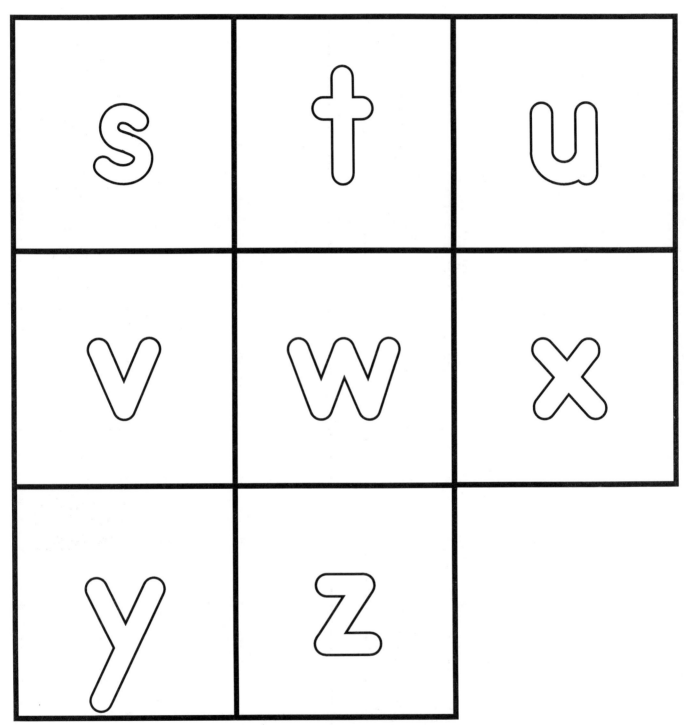

Phonemic Awareness © 1997 Creative Teaching Press

We Are Family

Student Name _____ **Date** _____

cake
bake
rake
lake

can
pan
man
fan

coat
goat
boat

hose
nose
rose

We Are Family

Student Name _____ **Date** _____

top
hop
mop
stop

ice
mice
dice
rice

train
rain
chain

gate
plate
skate

Phonemic Awareness © 1997 Creative Teaching Press

Letter Patterns

cat	did	lit	pop	set
kit	wet	jot	mug	vat
kid	dug	mitt	rid	tub
ten	bat	lot	pen	fox
top	fit	pit	rot	tug
pet	get	met	sat	yet
wax	hug	net	pig	bit
pot	got	pat	rug	cot
cub	hat	men	rub	den
fat	hop	rat	sit	bet
bug	jet	not	tax	hit
hen	ax	mop	tot	jug

Phonemic Awareness © 1997 Creative Teaching Press

Slip and Slide

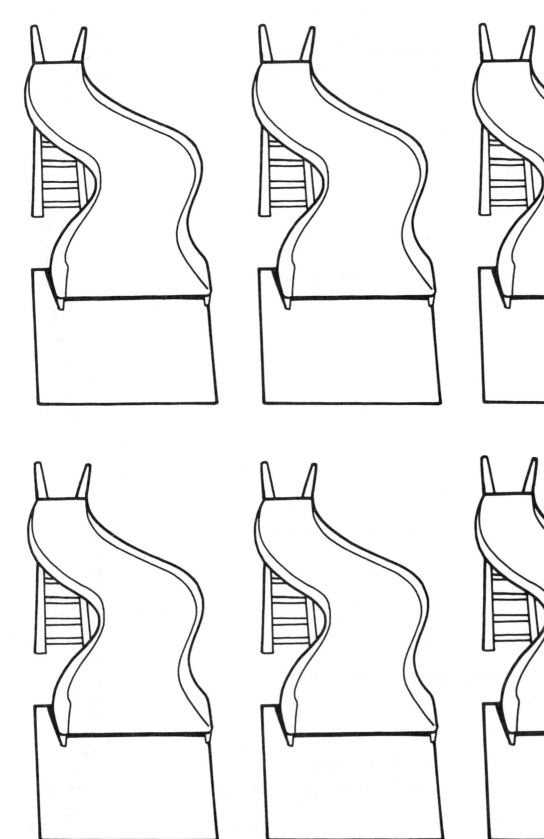

Phonemic Awareness © 1997 Creative Teaching Press

Build a Word—Teacher's Script

Directions: Have students build words using letter cards as you read the following directions aloud. Offer prompts when needed. Letters needed for this lesson: *t, a, n, i, g, s*

Take two letters and make the word *it*.

Now change one letter to make the word *at*.

Add one letter to make the word *ant*.

Without adding or taking away any letters, see if you can make a new word. (Tell younger students the word—*tan*.)

Now change one letter and rearrange others to make the word *sat*.

Change just one letter to make the word *sag*.

Once again, without adding or taking away letters, see if you can make a new word. (Tell younger students the word—*gas*.)

Now take away the *s* and the *a*, leaving only the *g*, and add two letters to make the ending sound –*ing*.

Now add another letter to make the word *sing*.

Add one more letter to make the word *sting*.

Take the *g* away, and add another letter to make the word *stain*. (Tell students they will need to move one letter to a new spot.)

Move the letters around to make a new word. (Tell younger students the word—*saint*.)

Now that we've made these different words, can anyone make a word that uses all six letters? Here are some clues: It's something really, really big, and it has the word *ant* in it.

(Answer: *giants*)

Recommended Books

Alliterations

A My Name Is Alice by Jane Bayer (Dial)

ABC of Monsters by Deborah Niland (McGraw)

Alfred's Alphabet Walk by Victoria Chess (Greenwillow)

Alligators All Around by Maurice Sendak (HarperCollins)

Alpha Beta Chowder by Jeanne and William Steig (HarperCollins)

Animalia by Graeme Base (Abrams)

Aster Aardvark's Alphabet Adventures by Steven Kellogg (Morrow)

Faint Frogs Feeling Feverish by Lilian Obligado (Viking)

Have You Ever Seen . . . ? by Beau Gardner (Dodd)

Six Sick Sheep: 101 Tongue Twisters by Joanna Cole (Morrow)

Rhymes

Across the Stream by Mirra Ginsburg (Greenwillow)

Animal Homes by Brian Wildsmith (Oxford)

The Annotated Mother Goose: Nursery Rhymes Old and New by William and Ceil Baring-Gould (Potter)

At the Crack of the Bat by Lillian Morrison (Hyperion)

Bears by Ruth Krauss (Harper)

Bears in Pairs by Niki Yektai (Bradbury)

Carrot/Parrot by Jerome Martin (Simon & Schuster)

Drummer Hoff by Barbara Emberley (S&S Trade)

Each Peach Pear Plum by Janet and Allan Ahlberg (Viking)

Father Fox's Pennyrhymes by Clyde Watson (Scholastic)

The Foot Book by Dr. Seuss (Random House)

Goodnight Moon by Margaret Wise Brown (Harper)

Have You Seen Birds? by Joanne Oppenheim (Scholastic)

Hide and Snake by Keith Baker (Harcourt)

Hop on Pop by Dr. Seuss (Random House)

Horton Hears a Who! by Dr. Seuss (Random House)

A House Is a House for Me by Mary Ann Hoberman (Viking)

Hunches in Bunches by Dr. Seuss (Random House)

The Hungry Thing by Jan Slepian and Ann Seidler (Scholastic)

I Can Read with My Eyes Shut by Dr. Seuss (Random House)

I Was Walking Down the Road by Sarah Barchas (Scholastic)

I Wish That I Had Duck Feet by Theo LeSieg (Random House)

In the Tall, Tall Grass by Denise Fleming (Holt)

Is Your Mama a Llama? by Deborah Guarino (Scholastic)

Jamberry by Bruce Degen (Harper)

Jessie Bear, What Will You Wear? by Nancy Carlstrom (Macmillan)

The Lady with the Alligator Purse by Nadine Westcott (Little, Brown)

More Spaghetti, I Say! by Rita Gelman (Scholastic)

Mother Goose: A Collection of Classic Nursery Rhymes by Michael Hagu (Holt)

A Mouse in My Roof by Richard Edwards (Doubleday)

On Beyond Zebra! by Dr. Seuss (Random House)

One Sun by Bruce McMillan (Holiday House)

Pickles Have Pimples and Other Silly Statements by Judi Barrett (Atheneum)

Play Day: A Book of Terse Verse by Bruce McMillan (Holiday House)

Possum Come a-Knockin' by Nancy Van Lann (Knopf)

Red Dragonfly on My Shoulder by Sylvia Cassedy and Kunihiro Suetake (HarperCollins)

The Shape of Me and Other Stuff by Dr. Seuss (Random House)

Sheep in a Jeep by Nancy Shaw (Houghton Mifflin)

Sheep, Sheep, Sheep, Help Me Fall Asleep by Arlene Alda (Delacorte)

Silly Sally by Audrey Wood (Harcourt)

Sing Hey Diddle Diddle: 66 Nursery Rhymes with Their Traditional Tunes
     by Beatrice Harrop (Sterling)

Strawberry Drums by Adrian Mitchell (Delacorte)

Street Rhymes Around the World by Jane Yolen (Wordsong)

There's a Wocket in My Pocket by Dr. Seuss (Random House)

Tickle-Toe Rhymes by Joan Knight (Franklin Watts)

To the Moon and Back by Nancy Larrick (Delacorte)

Tomie dePaola's Mother Goose by Tomie dePaola (Putnum)

The Wind Blew by Pat Hutchins (Macmillan)

Songs and Chants

And the Green Grass Grew All Around: Folk Poetry from Everyone by Alvin Schwartz
     (HarperCollins)

Anna Banana: 101 Jump-Rope Rhymes by Joanna Cole (Morrow)

Arroz Con Leche: Popular Songs and Rhymes from Latin America by Lulu Delacre (Scholastic)

Baby Beluga by Raffi (Crown)

Buffalo Girls by Bobette McCarthy (Crown)

Butterscotch Dreams by Sonja Dunn (Heinemann)

The Cat Who Loved to Sing by Nonny Hogrogian (Knopf)

Down by the Bay by Raffi (Crown)

Eency Weency Spider by S. Schindler (Bantam)

Frog Went A-Courting by Wendy Watson (Lothrop)

Go Tell Aunt Rhody by Aliki (Macmillan)

Hand Rhymes by Marc Brown (E.P. Dutton)

I Know an Old Lady Who Swallowed a Fly by Nadine Westcott (Little, Brown)

I Made a Mistake by Miriam Nerlove (Atheneum)

If You're Happy and You Know It by Nicki Weiss (Greenwillow)

In a Cabin in a Wood by Darcie McNally (E.P. Dutton)

Juba This and Juba That by Virginia Tashjian (Little, Brown)

Mary Wore Her Red Dress by Merle Peek (Clarion)

Miss Mary Mack by Joanna Cole (Morrow)

Oh, A-Hunting We Will Go by John Langstaff (Atheneum)

Old MacDonald Had a Farm by Tracey Pearson (Dial)

Peanut Butter and Jelly by Nadine Westcott (E.P. Dutton)

The Playtime Treasury by Pie Corbett (Doubleday)

Roll Over by Merle Peek (Houghton Mifflin)

Shake My Sillies Out by Raffi (McKay)

She'll Be Comin' 'Round the Mountain by Robert Quackenbush (Lippincott)

Shimmy Shimmy Coke-Ca-Pop! by John and Carol Langstaff (Doubleday)

Singing Bee! A Collection of Favorite Children's Songs by Jane Hart (Lothrop)

Skip to My Lou by Nadine Westcott (Little, Brown)

Teddy Bear, Teddy Bear: A Classic Action Rhyme by Michael Hague (Morrow)

There's a Hole in the Bucket by Nadine Westcott (HarperCollins)

This Old Man by Carol Jones (Houghton Mifflin)

Tingalayo by Raffi (Crown)

The Wheels on the Bus by Harriet Ziefert (Random House)

The Zebra-Riding Cowboy: Folk Songs from the Old West by Angela Medearis (Holt)